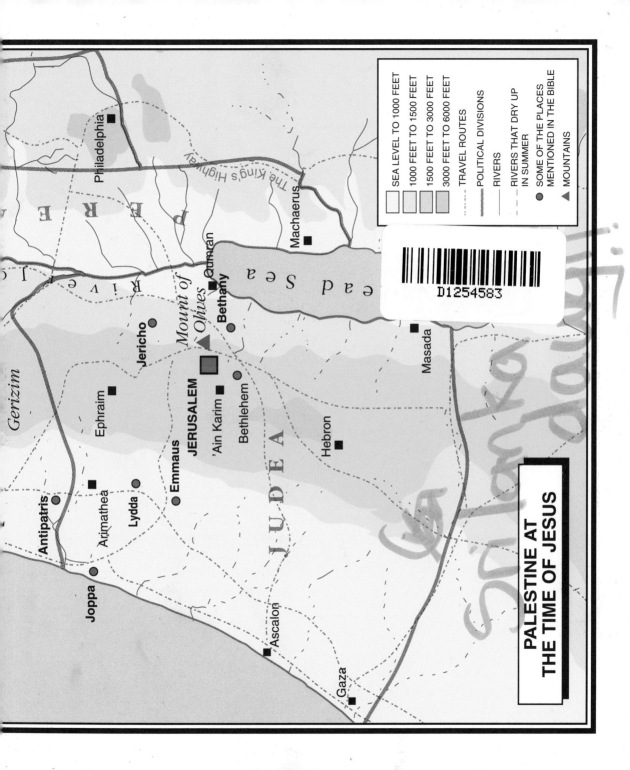

PALESTINE AT
THE TIME OF JESUS

SEA LEVEL TO 1000 FEET
1000 FEET TO 1500 FEET
1500 FEET TO 3000 FEET
3000 FEET TO 6000 FEET
------- TRAVEL ROUTES
POLITICAL DIVISIONS
RIVERS
----- RIVERS THAT DRY UP
IN SUMMER
● SOME OF THE PLACES
MENTIONED IN THE BIBLE
▲ MOUNTAINS

Philadelphia

The King's Highway

P E R E A

Qumran

Machaerus

Mount of Olives

Bethany

D1254583

D e a d   S e a

Jericho

Gerizim

Masada

Ephraim

JERUSALEM

'Ain Karim

Bethlehem

J U D E A

Hebron

Emmaus

Antipatris

Arimathea

Lydda

Joppa

Ascalon

Gaza

#20

Year 5

May We be One

English Canadian Catechetical Series

BORN *OF THE* **SPIRIT**

CANADIAN CATECHETICAL PROGRAM

CCCB

Contents

Canadian Conference of Catholic Bishops
Conférence des évêques catholiques du Canada

Dear Students:

I am delighted to present you with your new book, which is called *May We Be One*. This title comes from the words Jesus spoke to his disciples on the night before he died: "As you, Father, are in me and I am in you, may they also be one in us." This is Jesus' intention as he faces death. He wants his disciples to be one as he and his Father are one.

The next day Jesus died to make us one. Jesus offered his life for you, for me and for all people, so that we could live in union with God and with one another, in this world and forever. This is why the action of God in Jesus is called "Good News." It is the best news of all!

Now, when you were baptized, Jesus made you a member of his Church, which is his Body in the world. Just as we speak and act through our bodies, so does Jesus. And so, Jesus continues to speak and to make this "Good News" real through his Body in the world.

I am praying that you will come to know Jesus better this year, that you will remember always that he died for you and that he has made you a member of his Body in the world.

Jesus is your very best friend. He will never let you down.

Loving Peace and Care
in Jesus the Lord,

Most Rev. Eugene J. Cooney
Bishop of Nelson

Unit 1
The Church proclaims the good news

Theme 1 We are God's work of art
Theme 2 God has no favourites
Theme 3 May they all be one

1 We are God's work of art

"Hi. My name is Anna. My wish for our class is that we will make lots of friends."

Naming Game

Students gather in a circle.
First student begins.

Hi. My name is Anna.
My wish for our class is that
we will make lots of friends.

Next student shares.

Hi. My name is Lawrence.
My wish for our class is that
we will play lots of music
and sing lots of songs. And
this is Friendly Anna.

Lawrence touches Anna on the shoulder as she repeats his name.
The next student shares.

Hi. My name is Christopher.
My wish for our class is that we will plan some field trips together this year.

touching Lawrence on the shoulder

And this is Musical Lawrence and
Friendly Anna.

What is your wish for the year?
Do you remember the wishes of
your friends?

To welcome is to listen
to respect
to make an effort to get to know one another better
to help each other feel comfortable in a group

Spin a wheel of welcome!

"Hi. My name is Grant. Here is my spiral welcome wheel with my story of welcome."

 What story of welcome do you wish to tell? Make your own spiral welcome wheel by following the steps outlined on blackline master no. 1.

Share your story of welcome. Hang the spirals all around.

What's inside a rock?

Did you know that the earth is a giant ball of rock? Once a year (about every 365 ¼ days) it whirls an orbit around the sun. Our moon, too, is a great ball of rock. It circles around the earth.

Rocks are made up of mixtures of minerals. They are solid, with particles held firmly together. It takes millions of years for most rocks to form. **Geologists** divide them into three types based on the way they form:

Igneous rocks form when hot molten lava from the earth's centre cools and hardens. The cooling sometimes happens beneath the earth's surface, and the process is long and slow. The cooling may also take place on the earth's surface through volcanoes or cracks in the earth.

Most **sedimentary** rocks form in water. When rivers flow into lakes and seas, they carry with them a variety of sediments: mud, silt, sand, and pebbles. The particles eventually settle to the bottom. Over millions of years, layers of those sediments build up and cement together to form rock.

Metamorphic rock is made up of igneous and sedimentary rocks that have been forced together by great heat and pressure to form a new kind of rock.

Whatever their origin, rocks go through a hardening process and come together in solid form.

The process of making friends can be compared to the process of rock formation. Think about it. It takes time and effort to develop friendships. Once formed, however, friendships are solid, like rock.

8

Mother's Day

One afternoon in May 1973, five-year-old Richard came bounding in through the back door. He carried a carefully wrapped package. His bright eyes reflected the broad smile that lit up his little face. "I made this for you, Mom," he said, as he proudly handed me the package.

It was Mother's Day weekend. This was the carefully guarded secret he had been working on all week at school.

Inside was a rock, painted and decorated in a splatter paint design. How proud I felt that such a young child would spend so many hours preparing this special gift for his mom.

My rock became part of our household and a family conversation piece. I found many uses for this special rock. It was packed with our belongings in three moves we made over the years. Once, one of my children remarked, "You really do like that rock, Mom. You always bring it with you when we move."

I treasured the gift. Sixteen years later I realized just how precious the rock was to me. I was caring for my three-year-old grandson. He was playing with my rock and dropped it. Part of the rock cracked and chipped away. My heart seemed to sink as I picked up the pieces and thought about gluing them back in place. Just then I realized what the rock meant. I did not glue the pieces in place. I didn't have to.

The rock symbolized the strong love and bond between mother and child, between Richard and me. It symbolized life itself.

At times in our life we may feel neglected, forgotten or broken. But like the rock, our strength is in what we are, and in what we stand for.

Today my chipped rock is as important to me as it was that very special day in 1973. I treasure the moment when I hugged and thanked a loving five-year-old for a Mother's Day gift that will last a lifetime.

God's friendship with us is rock. In the Bible, God tells us that this friendship has been forming for a long, long time and will last forever!

Open your bible to Psalm 18. See how many rock words you can find. Write your favourite verse in your treasure book.

Rock treasures!

Do you have a special rock?

Bring it to class to share with your friends.

Create a rock display.

Let's go on a rock hunt!

Prepare for a rock hunt to find a rock for your class. Use the checklist to help plan your trip.

Checklist for the journey...
✔ Pick a location
✔ Choose a time
✔ Arrange transportation
✔ Get provisions
✔ Discuss the kind of rock you want for the class

Characteristics to look for:

size	colour
shape	smell
weight	texture

What kind of rock might best reflect God's friendship with us?
- our friendship
- unity and solidarity
- togetherness
- community built on rock

Have fun on your trip!

I am a rock!

My name is Rocky. I am full of colours. I have some red, brown and black dots all over my skin. I have little holes in me that were made by the sea.

I travelled in the sea for a long time. I have seen all kinds of fish and sea plants. Once I decided to go onto the nearest beach to play with the other rocks in the sand. There, I received the visit of a crab under me.

One day, a boy picked me up and put me on a log with a few of my friends. I was chosen by a class to be their pet rock! Since that day I have been sitting next to a candle and a book, on a table in a classroom. I have become a friend.

Melanie

In the midst of the land of silence – as I made a place for myself, as those who wore me down passed by – I knew that their footsteps many times may follow different roads. Many of the people avoid me as a solid little rock. As I grow old there is no promise that life lives up to my hopes. As the rain flows freely in the greyness of the sky that hangs low, making my beautiful colours sparkle brightly, I am still sad. The days turn into nights, turn the stars and bring the seasons.

All of a sudden it happened! I saw a little girl with a box, picking up rocks. I sparkled with joy, wishing that the little girl would collect me. It happened! The soft, gentle, warm touch of a little hand picked me up and placed me in a box. She looked at me for a long time. Then suddenly she had fallen over a stick. I stumbled out of the box and landed beside the grass. The little girl lay there crying.

Then I heard an older voice calling out, "Crystal!" The only thing I could do was sparkle by the brightness of the sun. My idea worked. The little girl was found by her father. Crystal's father picked me up and brought me home with them. Now they treasure me.

William

My name is Pebby Lewis. For years I have lived on a roadside near a big white fence. One September evening a young girl climbed over the fence. She was looking for a special rock.

All of a sudden she spotted me. Boy, was she excited! She picked me up, hugged me and raced home. Soon I was sitting in a pan getting my face washed. She examined me, looking carefully into my eye. She named me Pebby Lewis.

The next morning she took me to class and showed me to her friends. She said that I was the best rock in the whole wide world. I was happy when she said, "I love my rock."

Karen

I came from the sea, where the sun beat upon me, the waves crashed over me, and the salt water ate at me for a thousand years. Once I was more than a mile long – a century or two ago – but now I fit into my friend's small hand.

She found me on a rocky beach. I stood out looking nice, yelling out silently, "Choose me! Don't let me fade away into nothingness!" And so she did.

Lori

Hi! My name is Rocky. I'm a reddish, greenish, blackish, brownish rock. I've lived most of my life in the ocean, so it's not surprising that I have some cracks, chips and spots. Let me tell you my story.

One day, when I was a brand new rock, a glacier formed and pushed me down to the sea. My green spots came from grass that slid by. My brown spots came from clay that stuck to me. When I saw the ocean I was amazed at how big it was! I saw squid, trout, salmon, sharks, sunfish! Yes, even an occasional octopus! My black spots came from an oil spill. Boy, was I dirty! Most of the oil washed off. But some of it stayed.

I got my first crack from a very untidy tidal wave. I received my second crack from the wild wind who carried me along so fast that I hit another rock. I thought I had dissolved! Luckily, I only got a crack. I got my distinctive chip when a hurricane – of all things – threw me and I hit Bouldy, the boulder.

Then I washed up on a beach and a boy named Chris picked me. Two other boys carried me to Annunciation School. Here, I am the official Grade 5 class rock.

Michal

My name is Randi Rock. I like being a rock. I live in the Caribbean on the beach. When high tide comes in, I get covered with warm water. That's when my job starts. The fish use me as a marker so they know not to go in any farther. If low tide comes in, they will die on shore under the hot Caribbean sun.

My friends are Gertrude Gravel, Stephie Stone, Patricia Pebbles and Francie Flinstone. I am 10 years old and have a 5-year-old brother named Ricky Rock, and an 8-month-old sister named Rhonda Rock. My mother is Rebecca Rock and my father is Richard Rock.

My favourite rock group is the Beach Boys. My favourite magazine is The Rolling Stones. In the morning I sit in my rocking chair and munch on my favourite Rocky Road cereal. My favourite thing to do is rock 'n' roll. Well, it's time to dive now. It's almost high tide! Cheerio!

Stephanie

Imagine you are the class rock. Write your story in your treasure book.

Share it with your friends.

Celebrating our friendship!

Opening prayer

We gather to celebrate and thank God for the gift of each person in our classroom community.

Let us pray.

Silence

O God, giver of all good gifts,
you are the source of our life,
 our health, our gifts.
As we gather at the table of your word,
make us attentive to your voice
and alert to your presence.*
We ask this through our Lord Jesus Christ, your Son,
who lives and reigns with you in the unity of the Holy Spirit,
God for ever and ever.

Word of God

"We are God's work of art,
created in Christ Jesus
to live the good life
as from the beginning
God had meant us to live it."
(See Ephesians 2.10.)

Ritual action

May this rock be a sign of our togetherness.
Amen.

*[These two lines are from the Opening Prayer, Sixteenth Sunday of Ordinary Time, Year C, *Sunday Celebration of the Word and Hours*]

Closing prayer

Let us pray.

Silence

God of justice,
rock of our salvation,
open our minds and
    hearts to Jesus your Son.
Let us hold fast to
    his words
and express them in deeds,
that our faith be built on a
    sure foundation
and our lives be judged worthy of you.
Grant this through our Lord Jesus Christ,
    your Son,
who lives and reigns with you in the unity
    of the Holy Spirit,
God for ever and ever.*

*[This prayer is from the Ninth Sunday
of Ordinary Time, Year A,
Sunday Celebration of the Word and Hours]

Gather with your friends and plan a celebration of friendship and togetherness.

new words

geologist: a scientist who studies rocks
igneous: "fiery" or "of fire"
sedimentary: made up of sediments
metamorphic: means "change"

Remember

"We are God's work of art..."
(Ephesians 2.10)

2 God has no favourites

What do you remember most about your celebration of friendship?

Draw a picture of your favourite part in your treasure book. Share it at home.

David's rock

David sat at his desk by his bed and stared at the rock. It was a very plain rock about the size of a baseball. In bright gold letters it sported the words "GRANDFATHER AND DAVID 1996". It was Saturday and David was really missing his grandfather. They had been pals. As he held the rock, David remembered another Saturday almost a year ago.

It was a sunny day in June. Grandfather came for David as he usually did on Saturday. "Today, David, I am going to take you to a special place. So get ready for a long bus ride." Grandfather no longer drove Daisy, his red station wagon. He often joked about having to retire Daisy because she was too old.

Together the two pals set out for the bus stop at the street corner. David was excited. He looked forward to his outings with his grandfather. He wondered where they were going this time. He smiled as he thought of the zoo, the museum and the ice cream shop. The ride was long. They had to change buses near the arena. Where are we going, David thought, as he watched out the bus window.

After what seemed like five hours, Grandfather pushed the stop button. David pressed his face to the window one more time. He still did not know where they were.

There were no houses, just a lot of grass and bushes along the road. Yet somehow it seemed familiar. David and his grandfather moved toward the exit. When the bus door opened, David knew where they were. He could smell it! "We are at the beach," he exclaimed excitedly. I can smell the sea!" This was the best surprise! David loved the ocean. And all the happy times at the beach with his family popped into his mind. David looked up at his grandfather and saw the round, smiling face, the white hair and the blue eyes. He felt safe and happy.

David was bubbling with excitement as they walked over the hill and down to the seaside. "Tell me a story," David asked. His grandfather always told interesting stories when they walked. "David, I have a different story for you today," Grandfather said. "I brought you here because of all the places we have been, the beach is special. When you were just a baby, we would come here often. I would swoop you up in the air so that your face would catch the sea air. Then down you would go, splashing your feet in the waves. Even as a baby, you loved the sea. This is where we became best pals and where we shared our happiest outings. And like the sea, the sand and the rocks, our memories will last forever." Grandfather bent down and picked up a rock. He placed the rock in David's small hands. "See this rock, David. It will last for a long, long time. It is smooth because it has been washed by the waves for years and years. It will be here long after I am gone."

David was beginning to feel a little uncomfortable. He had never thought of his grandfather leaving. Slowly David began to understand Grandfather's story. He remembered how Jimmy Tallover's grandfather had died last winter. David felt like crying! "David," Grandfather said, "we love each other very much and we will be best pals forever just like that rock in your hand is forever. When we go home today we will put our names on the rock. Whenever you hold it, you will always remember our good times together."

Though he missed his best pal, David felt good inside as he held the rock. He remembered his grandfather and saw him in his mind just like that day at the beach: the round, smiling face, the white hair and the blue eyes. David felt safe and content.

"I love you, Grandfather," he whispered, "and I will always remember."

What was gathered together in David's rock? What is gathered in your class rock?

17

The Captain's Faith

The scene is set in the home of Cornelius, a captain in the Roman army. The set can be framed with curtains. Entrances are on the left and the right. The one on stage right leads to the outside; the one on the left leads to the interior of the house. Furniture may consist of some hassocks and a low sofa. In centre stage rear, there is a small pillar on which a small lamp burns.

As the curtain rises, the stage is empty. After a few seconds, Cornelius enters from stage left. He is carrying a small scroll. He is dressed in a Roman uniform.

Cornelius:
Flavius, Flavius, where are you?

Flavius: *(enters from stage right)*
Yes, master, what is it?

Cornelius:
Is there no sign of Sergeant Lucillus and my visitors yet?

Flavius:
Master, there is a group approaching the house from the direction of Joppa.

Cornelius:
That must be them. Call the household at once.

Flavius:
Yes, master, at once.
(Exit stage left.)

Cornelius:
Lord, I have done what you told me. I have sent to Joppa to ask this Simon Peter to come here. I ask only that you will give me the courage to do what you desire.

Claudia: *(enters from stage right)*
Flavius says your visitors are coming.

Cornelius:
Yes. Simon Peter will tell me what the Lord wishes me to do.

Claudia:
You were always a religious man, Cornelius. I can remember when you borrowed those Jewish scrolls from my father's library in Rome.

He thought it was strange reading material for a Roman officer.

Cornelius:
It was in those Jewish scrolls that I came to know the one true God. What fools we Romans are to worship a mere person like Caesar. The God who made us all must be greater than we are, and there is no such god in Rome.

Claudia:
I remember the day you removed all our household gods.

Cornelius:
Yes, and left the lamp burning to remind us all of the God of the Jewish people. I am so happy this visitor is coming to tell us more about this God.

(There is a sound of voices offstage right, and a Roman soldier enters followed by Simon Peter and two companions.)

Lucillus: *(saluting Cornelius in the customary Roman fashion by bringing his right arm across his chest)* Sir, here is your respected visitor and his companions.

Cornelius:
Thank you, Lucillus. *(Cornelius falls to his knees.)* Sir, you are most welcome to my home, you and your companions.

Simon Peter: *(raising Cornelius from his knees)* Get up! I am only a man myself.

Cornelius:
What can I do to make your stay comfortable?

Simon Peter:
You must know that it is not proper for a Jew to associate with a Gentile or have dealings with him.

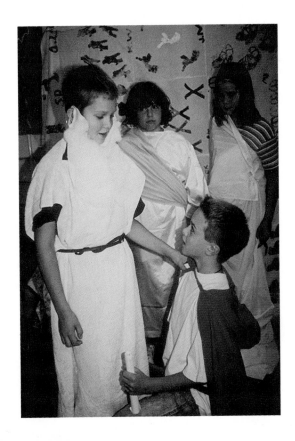

The Lord, however, has made it clear to me that no one can be called "unclean." That is why I have come in answer to your request. You will have to tell me what it is you want.

Cornelius:
I have long studied the religious scrolls of the Jews, and I have worked hard to keep the two great commandments of the Law by loving God and my neighbour. The other day while I was praying, a voice told me to send for you and gave exact directions where you were to be found.

Simon Peter:
Yes, and while I was at prayer the Lord gave me a vision of many kinds of food, some of which are unclean to us Jews. When the Lord told me to eat, I refused because I have always observed our laws. But the Lord told me that nothing which

God makes can be called unclean. Just as the vision ended, your sergeant and your servants came seeking me, and I remembered what the Lord had said. So here I am.

(While Peter is speaking, Claudia sits on a hassock, as does Lucillus. The servants gather in a group, stage right rear.)

Cornelius:
You will notice that my household has assembled. I am sure they will all find your words interesting. My wife, Claudia, shares my interest in the God of the Jews.

Simon Peter:
I have seen today that God has no favourites, but that anyone, of any nation or race, who acts in an upright manner, is acceptable to God. That good news has been given to us by Jesus Christ.

Cornelius:
You mean that Jewish prophet whom Pontius Pilate had executed?

Sergeant:
I knew that man was innocent, but Pilate was too afraid to let him go.

Simon Peter:
Well, you must all know the stories about Jesus, how he healed the sick, cast out devils, and preached the Good News of forgiveness for sin!

Cornelius:
Why, then, was he crucified?

Simon Peter:
The High Priest handed him over to be crucified. But God raised Jesus from the dead.

Claudia:
There was talk of some people stealing the body of Jesus from the tomb. But you say he rose from the dead?

Simon Peter:
The Jews tried to bribe the soldiers to say that we, his disciples, stole the body while they slept.

Cornelius:
No amount of money would be enough to bribe a Roman soldier to say he slept on duty.

Sergeant:
Right, Sir.

Simon Peter:
We are the witnesses to his resurrection. We walked with him, talked with him, and ate with him after the resurrection. Before he ascended into heaven, he sent us to baptize and to preach God's forgiveness for sin. We bear witness that Jesus will come back at the end of time to judge the living and the dead.

Cornelius:
You speak of Baptism, my friend. I believe that is the reason why God has sent you to me. I wish to be baptized, as does my wife and the rest of my household.

(There is a chorus of "I believe and I want to be baptized" from members of the group.)

Simon Peter:
I can see the Holy Spirit at work here today.

1st companion:
But Simon, they are Gentiles!

2nd companion:
What will the Church in Jerusalem say if you baptize them?

Simon Peter:
It matters little what they say. Can you not see that the Holy Spirit has come down upon them just as the Spirit came down upon us?

Can you not see how they praise God? Who could refuse to baptize them?

My friends, prepare to be baptized in the name of Jesus Christ. Indeed, God has no favourites!

(The scene closes with Simon, Cornelius and the others forming a circle. They raise their arms in praise, then break circle and face the audience. In unison, they repeat, "Yes, God has no favourites.")

What was Peter's discovery?

Design a bookmark with Peter's message on it for your treasure book.

Through Peter's eyes

Adam: Come on! I have the ball. Let's go play.

Sonya: Yeah, let's pick sides. I get Gary, Amanda and Eric on my team.

Adam: That's not fair! I only have two other people on my team.

Sonya: There's the new boy in class. You can ask him.

Adam: No way! Have you seen him? He's always tripping. He can't even hold the ball the right way. Besides, he said that they don't play baseball in his country.

Sonya: Yeah, but everyone deserves a chance.

Adam: I guess you're right. I'll pick him for my team and we'll teach him how to play.

What are the similarities between this role play and Peter's discovery?

Gather with your friends and create similar role plays based on real-life situations.

Remember

"The truth I have now come to realize is that God does not have favourites, but that anybody of any nationality who...does what is right is acceptable to God." (See Acts 10.34-35.)

3 May they all be one

You are in the marketplace in a small town in Galilee. You look around at all the displays. Can you smell the food? Do you see the different wares? The animals?
At the corner of the market,
near the synagogue,
you notice the man that everyone
has been talking about.
Jesus of Nazareth is standing at the well
and a crowd is gathering around him.
As you join the crowd, you hear Jesus tell
one of his parables:
"Which one of you having a hundred
sheep and losing one of them, does not
leave the ninety-nine in the wilderness
and go after the one that is lost until he
finds it? When he has found it, he lays
it on his shoulders and rejoices...."
It is quiet as Jesus finishes.
There is an excitement in the air.
Jesus talked so beautifully about God.
His picture of God carrying the
stray sheep
back to the sheepfold struck a deep
chord with everyone.
Jesus' God is so welcoming.

No one seems left out, no one is excluded.
Everyone is happy as they drift away
back to the stalls of the market. You are
happy, too.
You slowly open your eyes and
look around at your classmates.

**Take some quiet time to sketch
a picture in your treasure book
of God's dream of gathering:
"May they all be one..."
(John 17.21).**

No Translation Needed

My name is Joey and I am about your age. I live in a very cold part of Canada, in the North West Territories. Part of every year, my family moves out into the bush. Here I have learned many things from my father. He has shown me how to hunt for rabbits, lynx, fox, marten, beaver. I have learned how to ice-fish. I find this interesting and fun.

In the late fall when the ice is setting on the big lake, we go out to set the nets under the ice. Using an ice chisel we cut a hole in the ice. Then we pass a line attached to a long pole and propel it as far as we can. We look through the ice to see where it has landed. Here, we dig another hole and propel the pole farther along. Then we attach the net to the string. The net has been carefully prepared with floats on the top and rocks on the bottom to weight it down. Pulling the string along, the net takes its place under the ice.

Every four or five days we go out to check the nets. This is always fun, because I get to ride on the snowmobile. During the different months we catch white fish, suckers, and grailings. I have been helping my father fish for as long as I can remember – probably since I was 4 years old. We always buy our new nets at the general store. When they are torn my dad and mom mend them.

One night I went to a church meeting with my parents. Bishop Croteau and Sister Thompson were visiting each place in our diocese. The meeting was long because each time anyone spoke, there needed to be a translation. The bishop and sister didn't speak our language.

At the very end, Sister stood up and brought something out of a plastic bag. It was a fishing net. She didn't say anything, but held it up for us to see. The room came alive. There were big smiles on people's faces, especially the elders.' Some of them were making motions with their hands. They were saying, "Making nets" in our language. The Sister said, "No translation is needed."

I wondered what she meant. Then someone read the story about Peter fishing all night and catching nothing (Luke 5.1-11). I couldn't imagine it, really, because when we went fishing we always caught something.

Then Sister explained how we were making this net as a diocese. Each community made a row, using a different colour. We were going to be green. Of course, one row would never catch a fish. The net wasn't big enough yet. Working together, though, we would eventually have a good fishing net. We would be like the apostles, "catching people."

I was amazed at the excitement in the room. Who would do our row? I moved closer to Sister and the bishop because I wanted to see. We had always bought our nets. I had never seen anyone make one. Several older men and women knew how. Others pointed to them. The two men got up and started making our row. It went so quickly! They used a little wooden block to make sure all the holes were the same size. They wrapped the string around it and then used a wooden needle to tie the knots. Their fingers seem to fly! One held the net taut and the other used the needle. Many others were pushing forward, watching and telling tales of making nets.

As I continued to watch, they put part of the net in my hand. "Hold tight, so that the holes will be even," they said. I was thrilled to be part of this net-making. I was so glad I had come.

As I skipped home, I remembered the words of Jesus to Peter: "Don't be afraid, Peter. Today you caught many fish. From now on, it is people you will be catching, inviting them to be my friends . . . to come follow me." I am eager to see the net again next year. By then, all 35 communities in our diocese will have added their rows!

What is gathered together in this story?
Why do people gather together?

A class begins a mosaic

Using special fabrics from home, students piece together a mosaic of memories. Tak a look at their creation on the next page.

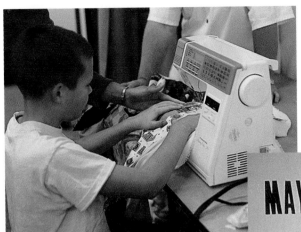
Stitching around fabric to create a mosaic

My dad used to be a basketball player. He played in the Olympics. This is a piece of his shorts. It makes me feel proud of him.
David

Showing off our mosaic!

This comes from a pillow made by Shannon's grandma. Once we used it to have a pillow fight. It reminds us that we are best friends.
Shannon and Shelby

This is from my mom's favourite dress when she was twenty. I chose it because I like to imagine what it looked like on my mom.
Katelyn

This fabric comes from my Christmas stocking when I was two. It is very special to me.
Matthew

Choose a special piece of fabric to add to your class mosaic.
Where would you like to place the mosaic when it is finished? Why?

Saint Francis Xavier

Francis tossed and turned all night. He was exhausted and wanted to sleep, but his mind was restless. Until the previous day, he had had definite plans for a great future. Now, he was no longer that certain.

Francis was a rich, energetic young man who loved the excitement of social life. He was a brilliant student, quite certain of a future career in a distinguished university. For him, all things pointed to a life of total happiness.

One day, Xavier met Ignatius Loyola, a young man studying for the priesthood. The two became close friends. Francis shared his dream of the future. Ignatius listened attentively and then asked a simple question: "Francis, if you live according to your plans, what good will you have done with your life?" That was the question that not only kept Francis awake; it made him aware that God might be inviting him to another kind of life.

Francis decided to join Loyola in a new religious order known as the Society of Jesus and became a missionary priest. He was ready to use his talents, energy and love of life to take the message of Christ to even the most distant regions of the world.

In 1540, Francis boarded a ship bound for India. It is hard to even imagine the hardships of this four-month journey.

In India, Francis went to colonies of settlers who had come from Europe. Some of them accepted and welcomed him. Others persecuted and even tried to kill him. They were angry because he challenged their way of living Christianity and particularly their involvement in the slave trade.

Francis loved the natives of India and travelled many miles to reach them. He always tried to be one with the people in the places he visited, living with the poorest and sharing their food and shelter. He had to learn many languages, which he found very hard. Many became Christians through his example, his concern for others and his preaching.

One day, Francis met a rich Japanese nobleman who was interested in becoming a Christian. This new friend invited Francis to come to Japan. He accepted the invitation gladly. In it, he saw a call from God to bring the good news to a region where the message had not yet been proclaimed.

In Japan, Francis had to adapt to a new way of living and learn another new language. He never spared himself, and through his missionary activities many became Christians.

While Francis was working in Japan, a new vision was taking shape in his mind: "China is so close . . . yet so far . . . I must go there . . . I must get to China . . . God, help me get to China. There are so many people waiting there."

He heard that a ship was leaving for China. Francis saw this as an opportunity to follow his dream. He was on his way. But this journey was never completed. Francis became very ill and the ship abandoned him on a desolate island on the coast of China. Here, his missionary journey was completed. He died on this island in 1551.

We celebrate the feast of St. Francis Xavier on December 3.

What do you think kept Francis going?

Was he a gatherer? How?

Together with your friends, research other missionary saints.
Choose favourite ways to tell your stories.

Remembering our stories!

What stories have you collected for your storytelling project so far? Do you have a favourite story?

Remember

May they all be one. Father, may they be one in us, as you are in me and I am in you, so that the world may believe it was you who sent me. (See John 17.21.)

Unit 2
The Church believes in the Lord Jesus

Theme 4 Peter shares his belief in the Lord Jesus
Theme 5 Baptized in the name of Jesus Christ
Theme 6 We proclaim the greatness of God

4 Peter shares his belief in the Lord Jesus

In a Grade 5 classroom in Goose Bay, Labrador, students gather around a young man in a wheelchair. A soft hush falls upon the room as he begins to tell his story to the class.

Hi! My name is Dwayne Compton. I'm 23 years old and I'm a quadriplegic. I wasn't always in a wheelchair. Once, I was just like you. I walked, ran, competed in sports and played hockey. But there's much more. Today I will share with you what I was like before my accident and the kind of person I am now.

As a teenager, I had a chip on my shoulder. I didn't care about people. I only cared about myself. I hated school and everything it had to offer. I wanted nothing to do with it. As time went on, my attitude worsened. I did drugs. I drank too much. I lied. I stole. I took everything and everyone for granted. Despite all the bad things in my life, however, I had one great love. It was sports. I loved going to the gym. I loved weight-lifting and exercising. Most of all, I loved hockey. Little did I think that what I loved best would turn out to hurt me the most.

On April 4, 1983, I was playing in a midget all-star hockey tournament in Goose Bay. In the second game, my whole life turned upside down. I slid headfirst into the boards, leaving my body completely helpless. I could not feel from the chest down. I could not move at all. I was like a balloon that was punctured on the ice.

I was taken from the arena to the hospital in an ambulance. I didn't know what was happening, but I knew something was seriously wrong on the inside. X-rays confirmed the worst and my parents were told the shocking news: "He'll never walk again. He'll be in a wheelchair for the rest of his life."

It was hard to imagine. Just weeks earlier I had been so strong and independent. I never dreamed that I would experience such a dramatic fall. Later I learned that it was for my own good.

I felt humble in my condition. Cards kept pouring in from across Newfoundland. People around me were kind, sympathetic and caring. And yet I lay broken-hearted on my bed. I cried from the bottom of my heart. It was the first real cry I had ever had.

Within a few weeks I began breathing on my own again. Slowly, I learned a whole new way of dealing with people. I saw how they cared for me. Gradually, I began to communicate. I began to say, "Thank you." It was a new experience in my life.

The biggest change came, however, after I left rehabilitation. It was March 1984. I returned home. I had to get to know my family in a whole new way. They had to learn how to wash me, dress me, feed me, how to put me in and out of the wheelchair. I began to see how much parents really love and care for their children. I was a full-time job and they faithfully accepted it.

Still there was work to be done in my heart. There was a constant longing for inner peace. In my quiet time I began to think about God. I felt that God was there guiding me. For the very first time I began to listen to the word of God in the gospel.

I began to see things in a new way. Jesus became a central part of my life. I was like a broken vessel that had to be molded again – one day at a time.

It was as if there were two different people, an old Dwayne and a new Dwayne. The new Dwayne was beginning to learn what it means to care about people. No matter what a person does – love that person. No matter what a person is – love that person. The wheelchair had become an instrument to

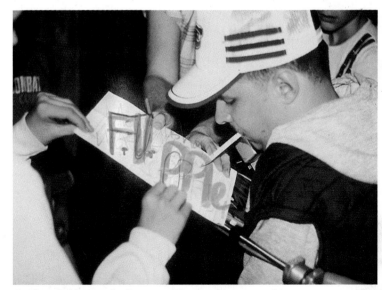

Students hold paper for Dwayne as he signs his name to his story.

help me see the truth in the things around me, to show me what I had taken for granted.

So as you look at me here today, paralyzed in this wheelchair, don't think of all that I have lost. Think of what I have gained. I now have a heart that cares about people. I know how to say "thank you." Yes, I still depend on my family and friends. But look at the relationship that I have with them now. I love them. Every day I thank God for the new relationships that are helping to mend and rebuild my life. Someday, by God's grace, I will walk again. For now I can only appreciate what has already been given to me.

How is Dwayne's story a story of change?

What is Dwayne's message?

Decide with your friends on a title for the story.

The poor belong to God

Sometimes it takes a shocking event to make us see things differently. That is what Bishop Paul Reding discovered. He had gone to San Salvador to attend the funeral of his friend Oscar Romero, a fellow bishop.

Oscar Romero was the bishop of San Salvador at a time when there was much violence in the country of El Salvador. His people were poor. A number of them had begun to demand that rich landowners give up parts of their land, so that the peasants (*campesinos*) might become farmers. The rich hardly used their land. When the demands went unheard, a terrible civil war broke out.

Bishop Romero took up the cause of the poor. He believed that Jesus would have done the same. "God," he preached, "has a special love for poor people and struggles with them. God wants poor people to have food, work, a home and a fair share of the land." Week after week on Sundays he would tell his people how the poor were suffering.

Oscar Romero paid dearly for his belief. One day, those who were angry at Bishop Romero for his sermons decided to silence him. They hired a killer. While celebrating the Eucharist at the altar one morning, Bishop Romero was shot and killed. Romero had become a martyr – a witness of God's love for the poor.

Bishop Reding had come all the way from Canada to pray that Romero's death would not be in vain. He and 100,000 other people crowded into the cathedral and spilled out into the square. They had come to say goodbye to their "saint." But the rich landowners and their government were afraid that more people would accept what Bishop Romero had stood for. During the funeral Mass, after the gospel, soldiers began to shoot from rooftops. They threw bombs among the people. Everyone panicked and fled to avoid the bullets. Bishop Reding was in the square. He scaled an iron fence and escaped into the cathedral. Forty people were killed and many more were wounded. Christian faith had claimed a few more witnesses.

The death and funeral of Archbishop Romero marked Bishop Reding deeply. He had gone to the funeral of his friend. He knew what his friend had stood for; he had always sided with the poor. But what came home to Bishop Reding was the risk. He had made only a small gesture of being present at the funeral. That was enough for him to be seen as dangerous. Without realizing it, he had become a witness to the truth of Archbishop Romero: the poor belong to God.

Bishop Reding came home to Canada with a deep need to tell this story. Wherever he went, the power of the story was felt. Like Peter, he too had realized something new.

Take this story of Bishop Reding home to share with your family.

Upon this rock

When Jesus came to the region of Caesarea Philippi he put this question to his disciples: "Who do people say the Son of Man is?" And they said, "Some say he is John the Baptist, some Elijah, and others Jeremiah or one of the prophets." "But you," he said, "who do you say I am?" Then Simon Peter spoke up. "You are the Christ," he said, "the Son of the living God." Jesus replied, "Simon son of Jonah, you are a happy man! Because it was not flesh and blood that revealed this to you but my Father in heaven. So I now say to you: "You are Peter and on this rock I will build my Church." (Matthew 16.13-18)

What does the word Peter mean?

Why do you think Jesus chose this name for Simon Peter?

Draw a picture of the event in your treasure book.

Add Peter's name to your class rock.

Design a banner with these words: "You are Peter and on this rock I will build my Church."

Hang it in your gathering space.

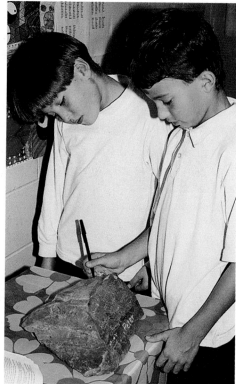

The Church is for all people

A circle of people

A Grade 5 class demonstrates how Jesus and his Church are for all people.

 Follow the directions on blackline master no. 4 and design your own circle of people. Write a message in the circle centre.

The Holy Spirit helps the Church to grow

The first references given here name the locations of early Church communities. The additional verses (given in brackets) provide a brief summary of what happened in each place. Take a tour through the places. Give an eyewitness account of the events.

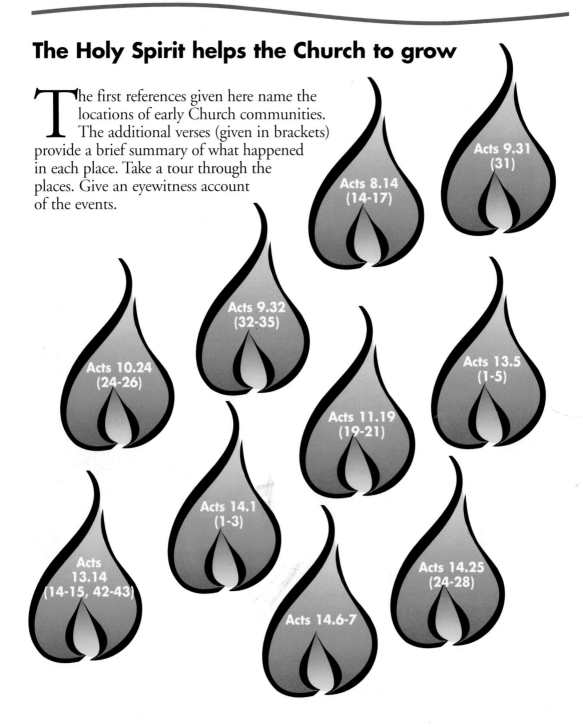

Acts 8.14 (14-17)

Acts 9.31 (31)

Acts 9.32 (32-35)

Acts 10.24 (24-26)

Acts 13.5 (1-5)

Acts 11.19 (19-21)

Acts 14.1 (1-3)

Acts 13.14 (14-15, 42-43)

Acts 14.6-7

Acts 14.25 (24-28)

38

Acts 16.12 (11-15)

Acts 17.1 (1-4)

Acts 17.10 (10-12)

Acts 18.1 (1-5)

Acts 19.1 (1-6)

Acts 28.14 (14-16)

WE ARE GODS WORK OF ART

new words

quadriplegic: a person whose four limbs are paralyzed

Peter: means "rock"

Remember

"...You are Peter and on this rock I will build my Church." (Matthew 16.18)

5 Baptized in the name of Jesus Christ

The man from Ethiopia

The apostle Philip was taking a detour down the desert road that goes from Jerusalem to Gaza. As he was walking along, the chief treasurer from the court of Queen Candace of Ethiopia came along in his chariot. He was on his way home to Ethiopia. The Spirit said to Philip, "Go up and meet that chariot." When he did this, Philip heard the man reading from the book of the prophet Isaiah.

Philip said to him, "Do you understand what you are reading?"

"How can I understand by myself?" replied the man. "Please sit beside me and explain it all."

So Philip did. As they drove along, he went on to tell the Good News of Jesus to the man.

After a while they came to some water. The man said, "Look, here is some water. Is there any reason why I shouldn't be baptized here and now?"

He stopped the chariot and they both went down into the water, where Philip baptized him.

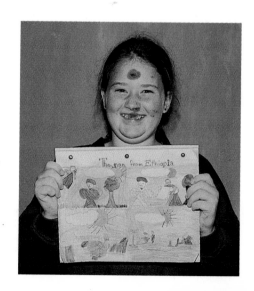

There are four key steps in this story. Can you find them?

Design a cartoon about the story for your treasure book. Share it with a friend and at home.

Give thanks to the Holy Spirit.
Pray the Holy Spirit prayer together:

V. Come, Holy Spirit, fill the hearts of your faithful.
R. And kindle in them the fire of your love.
V. Send forth your Spirit, and they shall be created.
R. And you will renew the face of the earth.

Let us pray

Lord,
by the light of your Holy Spirit
you have taught the hearts of your faithful.
In the same Spirit
help us to relish what is right
and always rejoice in your consolation.
We ask this through Christ our Lord. Amen.

An interview with a new Christian!

After celebrating the Easter Vigil, new Christians are called **neophytes**. The word neophyte means "newly planted." Here are some key questions that you might ask new Christians when they come to visit:

When did you hear the word of God?

Who told you about Jesus?

Who explained the Scriptures to you?

How has your life changed?

How are you witnessing to Jesus' presence?

Aurelia's initiation

Reporter 1: Here we are at the cathedral in Ravenna, in northern Italy. It's the year 450; things are relatively calm in the city these days. Christians are becoming more numerous now because there is much less danger of being persecuted for being a Christian than in the early days. I'm now standing in front of the baptistery, a building separate from the basilica. This place is soon going to see some important action.

Reporter 2: It's now 5 o'clock in the morning here in Ravenna, still dark at this time of year.

Well, here comes Aurelia with her mother and father. She is one of the elect.

"Good morning, Aurelia. How are you feeling at this moment?"

Aurelia: "Oh, I'm a little nervous. I couldn't sleep at all last night."

Reporter 2: "Would you tell the people back in Canada how at age 11 you decided to become a Christian?"

Aurelia: "Mom, Dad and I met this wonderful family one evening. They told us the story of Jesus. We wanted to hear more. For more than a year now

43

we have prepared ourselves for this day. We have come to realize that God loves all people and that God has shown this through Jesus."

Reporter 2: "Thanks, Aurelia. I hope everything goes well with you and your family."

Let's follow Aurelia into the baptistery.

Reporter 1: Here we are in the vestibule off to the side of the baptistery. Bishop Neon has just arrived. The elect are waiting with their godparents and sponsors.

Bishop Neon: "Elect, please remove your robes."

Reporter 2: This will give us a chance to tell you about the baptistery building itself.

Reporter 1: Beyond the door on my left is a magnificent room into which the elect will be admitted in a few moments. When the doors open, notice overhead a mosaic showing Jesus' own Baptism in the Jordan. Mosaics of the apostles surround the image of Jesus in the circular dome.

Bishop Neon: "Elect, face the west."

Reporter 2: Westward signifies darkness. The light of the sun will shortly appear from the east. In a moment the elect will be invited to turn away from darkness, sin, selfishness and death.

Bishop Neon: "Turn your backs now on the darkness and face east."

Reporter 2: Each candidate is rubbed with olive oil. Deaconesses do this for the women.

(a door opens vigorously)

Reporter 1: We are now able to see into the baptistery. Let's follow the elect, who have never seen the inside of this glorious room before. The bishop, priests, deaconesses and deacons are moving in with the elect. The floor sparkles with richly coloured tiles. There are oil lamps all around.

Reporter 2: Right here on my left is the baptismal pool. The sound of the water flowing reminds us of Psalm 42:

"As a doe longs for running streams, so longs my soul for you, my God."

Reporter 1: Bishop Neon is deep in prayer. He prays that God's Spirit may touch the waters and change them into waters of life. The bishop is now giving the water a few whacks with his staff, recalling how Moses struck the rock to bring forth the water of life.

Reporter 2: A deaconess has just gone down into the pool.

Let us watch Aurelia as she is being baptized.

Reporter 1: It looks like she is going to be the first to be baptized! She's just being led down into the water by a deaconess. You'll notice on your screen the ripples of colour on the water as her oily body descends into the pool.

Bishop Neon: "Aurelia, do you believe in God the Father, who created the heavens and the earth?"

Reporter 1: Aurelia, looking up at the bishop, says, "Yes, I do!" but she wasn't expecting the next move. The deaconess beside her pulled her backwards and she got a few gulps of water. But she is in good hands and is now standing upright again.

Bishop Neon: "Aurelia! Do you believe in Jesus Christ, the only Son of God, born of the Virgin Mary, who suffered under Pontius Pilate, died and was buried?"

Aurelia: "I do."

Reporter 2: Aurelia was ready this time and had her mouth shut!

Bishop Neon: "Aurelia! Do you believe in the Holy Spirit and the holy catholic Church, the communion of saints, the forgiveness of sins, the resurrection of the body and the life to come?"

Aurelia: "I do."

Reporter 2: Aurelia, after being briefly held under the water three times, is now being brought out of the pool and dried.

Reporter 1: Another helper is opening up a jar of perfumed oil. He is pouring it over Aurelia's head. This expensive oil is not spared. It is even running down over her body.

Reporter 2: We're sorry you can't smell the magnificent perfume in this oil, called chrism.

Reporter 1: The bishop just said, "Aurelia, servant of God, you are anointed in the name of the Father, the Son and the Holy Spirit."

Reporter 2: Aurelia is now being dressed in a white linen robe as the other baptisms continue. *(brief pause)*

Reporter 2: Hello again. The Easter hymn announcing the victory of Christ has just begun: "Christ is risen from the dead," it resounds. The baptisms are now completed and we are on our way to the church. We are being led by Bishop Neon.

Reporter 1: The bishop has just struck the church doors with his staff. The church doors open. The people celebrating the vigil have stopped and are welcoming the baptismal party with shouts of joy.

Reporter 2: Wow! This is more exciting than New Year's Eve celebrations! People are wild with joy as they shout "Jesus is risen!" and welcome in the newly baptized.

Each of the newly baptized, now dressed in white and carrying a lighted lamp, is walking toward the altar.

(all sing an Easter song here)

Reporter 1: Bishop Neon just made a beautiful fatherly gesture with his arms, welcoming these new Christians into the community. And everyone has burst out again with "Jesus is risen!"

Aurelia is now being brought forward to the bishop. He lays his hand on her head and signs her forehead with the cross.

Bishop Neon: "The servant of God is sealed with the Holy Spirit."

Everyone: "Amen"

Reporter 1: The bishop is now giving the kiss of peace to the new Christians and they are passing it on.

Reporter 2: This is incredible! People are weeping with joy. There's not a dry eye in this church!

Reporter 1: Bread and wine are now being brought to the holy table. Bishop Neon begins the prayer of the Eucharist.

Reporter 2: Aurelia is just now going forward to receive the body of Christ and to drink from the cup.

Reporter 1: We are told that this celebration will continue for 50 days. Unfortunately, we have to sign off now, but we just want you to see one last time this young girl, Aurelia, in her beautiful white baptismal robe. As a Christian, she has now put on Christ.

Reporter 2: Time to get back into our time machine and return to Canada. Happy Easter!

How is the event in this story similar to your Baptism? How is it different?

Design a cartoon about your Baptism in your treasure book.

46

The Apostles' Creed

I believe in God,
the Father almighty,
creator of heaven and earth.

I believe in Jesus Christ,
his only Son, our Lord.
He was conceived by the power
of the Holy Spirit
and born of the Virgin Mary.
He suffered under Pontius Pilate,
was crucified, died, and was
buried.
He descended to the dead.

On the third day he rose again.
He ascended into heaven,
and is seated at the right hand of
the Father.
He will come again to judge the
living and the dead.

I believe in the Holy Spirit,
the holy catholic Church,
the communion of saints,
the forgiveness of sins,
the resurrection of the body
and the life everlasting. Amen.

new words

elect: those who have celebrated the rite of election or enrollment of names in the Rite of Christian Initiation of Adults.

neophyte: person who is initiated through Baptism, Confirmation and the Eucharist in the Rite of Christian Initiation of Adults. The word comes from *Neos* (new) and *phuton* (a plant) in New Testament Greek.

Remember

The sacraments of initiation are Baptism, Confirmation and Eucharist.

6 We proclaim the greatness of God

Living water,
  like a river
like a fountain,
  like the sea.
Living water,
  like a river
ever rising,
  rise in me.

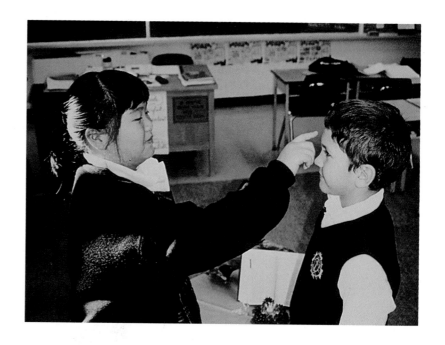

"Mark, I sign you with the sign of eternal life in the name of the Father and of the Son and of the Holy Spirit." Amen.

How was your water ritual similar to this one?

A teaching box

Get together with your friends and design a storytelling box on Baptism. Here is a list of things to highlight:

- the community gathers
- the word of God is proclaimed
- baptismal promises are renewed
- the sign of the cross is made on the forehead
- persons are baptized by pouring water or by immersion with these words: "I baptize you in the name of the Father and of the Son and of the Holy Spirit"
- being anointed with chrism
- white garments are put on
- a baptismal candle is lit from the Easter candle.

Tell the story with a series of drawings or flash cards. These could be placed on or inside the box. Collect photographs, a baptismal candle, a white garment and a baptismal certificate to put in the box. When it is completed, add the box to your storytelling centre.

Invite a group of young children to your classroom. Use your teaching box to show them what you have learned about Baptism. Use the guide on the next page to help lead them in prayer.

Share a story

In Baptism God's own life and love is poured into our hearts through the Spirit of Jesus.

Invite the children to listen to the story of Philip and the Ethiopian.

Sign each other with blessed water in the name of the cross.

Together sing "Living Water."

Use your teaching box to tell all about Baptism.

Burst a balloon

Add a favourite fragrance such as balsam or almond extract to a deflated balloon. Blow up the balloon to full size. Puncture the balloon. Absorb the fragrance as it fills the room.

Speak softly to the children

Relax. Close your eyes. Be very still and quiet.

Listen to the sounds around you. Listen.

(Pause)

Feel your breathing, in and out, in and out.

(Pause)

Now think of the words "Come, Holy Spirit." Say these words slowly, while you breathe in and out, in and out:

"Come, Holy Spirit. Come, Holy Spirit."

Open your eyes now and write the words "Come, Holy Spirit" on your paper, along with a prayer of your own.

Invite the children to share their prayers.

Remember

Baptism is the sacrament of new birth in the Holy Spirit.

Unit 3
The Church celebrates God's mighty deeds

Theme 7 We remember the risen Lord
Theme 8 We celebrate the breaking of the bread
Theme 9 We give praise and thanks to God

7 We remember the risen Lord

Jennifer's missed birthday

Jennifer loved birthdays, especially her own. This year, she began counting the days off exactly one month before the actual date!

The days seemed to speed up as her birthday drew near. The night before the big day, she made up her mind exactly what clothes she would wear. She laid them out on the table beside her bed. The red rolled collar sweater, which she reserved for special occasions, would surely bring a question from someone at the breakfast table. Just in case they forget, she thought.

Morning came and she hopped out of bed. She could almost hear herself say, "Happy birthday, Jennifer!" She dressed, grabbed her school things and hurried down to breakfast.

"Where's Mom?" she asked, as her older brother made his way to the table with a heaping plate of pancakes.

"She was called to work early," he replied. "But then she'll get to come home earlier too," he added.

"Good," said Jennifer, thinking of what her mom might have cooked up to surprise her. Yet she couldn't bring herself to mention her birthday. "It's a lot more fun when other people think of it," she whispered to herself as she scurried off to school.

Jennifer's best friends were all in class. She was sure that one of them would announce her birthday. She wondered who it would be. "Boy, is this weird," she thought to herself as the morning disappeared and nobody remembered. "Maybe they're just hiding it on purpose because they want to surprise me after school," she consoled herself as she sat at her desk. After all, they were talking about it yesterday!

The dismissal bell rang and Jennifer watched as the students scattered. "What are you doing after school?" her friend Lynn asked.

"Nothing much," Jennifer answered. She felt angry and hurt. It was hard to keep from saying something rude. "What about you?" she asked.

"I'm going over to Josie's place," Lynn said. "She's got a new puzzle that we're going to check out. See you tomorrow," she shouted as she rode off on her bicycle.

That did it! Jennifer knew for sure now that there was no surprise party coming from any of her friends. She walked home sad and hurt, wondering if Josie and Lynn were really her friends after all.

"They're great friends when I do things for them," she thought. "But maybe that's all."

As she came up the step, she was surprised to find the front door locked. "What next? Mom not home?" she uttered with big sigh. She was barely inside when the phone rang.

It was her mom's voice. "Jennifer, I have to stay at work till late tonight. One of the workers was hurt this afternoon and had to be taken to hospital.

"They asked me to take her place because I'm the only one on duty who knows her job. Happy birthday! Jennifer, I'm really disappointed that we can't be together tonight to celebrate. Maybe we can do something special Friday night. Is that okay?"

Jennifer was almost too shocked to say anything. She managed a weak "Thanks, Mom. I understand." She hung up the phone and disappeared into her bedroom for a good cry.

About five o'clock her brother called to her. "Jennifer, someone's here for you."

What a surprise when she came to the door! There was Josie leading a procession into the house, birthday cake in hand, 10 candles burning and everybody singing "Happy Birthday!" And guess who was at the end of the procession? Her mom!

They gathered around the kitchen table and Jennifer blew out the candles. (It took her three tries, she was so excited.) Lynn handed Jennifer a beautifully wrapped gift. As she took it, Jennifer remembered the word "puzzle." Sure enough, it was a new kind of game that her friends chose especially for her.

"But Mom," Jennifer asked, "how did you get here?"

"It was Karen's mom," she said. "When she heard I couldn't be at your party, she volunteered to take my place."

"I was sure I'd have no birthday party," said Jennifer, her eyes sparkling. "This is just the greatest birthday ever!"

What did Jennifer expect after her mother's call?

Why was she feeling sad and left out?

Do you think the party was even better than her highest hopes?

Do you have a story of surprise to share with your friends?

On Stage!

Scene 1: At the tomb
(Music plays softly in the background)
Three women are carrying their prepared spices to the tomb.

Mary Magdalene: Look! Look! The stone has been rolled away and the body of Jesus is gone!

Joanna: Oh, no! His body has been taken away.

Mary: Who would do such a thing?

First Angel: Do not be afraid. Why are you looking in the tomb for Jesus? Only dead people are in tombs.

Second Angel: Jesus is not here. He has risen just as he said he would.

Joanna: Let us leave this place. I am shivering with fright.

First Angel: Don't be afraid.

Second Angel: Go and tell the disciples to go to Galilee. There they will see him.

Mary: The Lord Jesus is alive! He is risen!

Scene 2: At the upper room

Peter: Andrew, do you often think about Jesus?

Andrew: I can't think of anything else. Some of his stories about God keep

going through my head. He could keep us listening to him for days.

Bartholomew: I can't forget how much good he did.

Thomas: How many sick people he cured! How many times he gave peace of mind to people!

Miriam: I was not always comfortable, especially when he asked us to go and visit those sinners and eat with them.

John: I guess he wanted us to know that God welcomes all people.

Philip: What wrong did he do to deserve to die on a cross? I just can't understand it.

Rachel: You don't think that they will come for us as well, do you?

James: Lock the doors and windows!

Philip: We can't stay here forever. When it is dark I will go back home. I will never forget him.

Peter: I'll wait awhile yet. Perhaps we should pray. God could not abandon such a just man.

Scene 3: The walk to Emmaus

Nathaniel: Cleopas, I feel so sad. I can't believe that all of this has come to an end.

Cleopas: It was hard to leave this morning. Everyone is afraid. Did you notice Peter crying?

Stranger: What are you talking about?

Cleopas: Are you the only visitor in this area who doesn't know the things that have been happening these last few days?

Stranger: What things?

Nathaniel: All about Jesus. Jesus was a great prophet. He proved it by the things he said and did before God and all the people. But last week he was condemned to death and he died on the cross.

Cleopas: All this happened two days ago. Nathaniel and I are on our way home.

Stranger: How foolish you are! If you would only believe what the prophets said about the Messiah, you would know that the Christ should suffer and so enter into his glory.

(Cleopas and Nathaniel look with wonderment at the stranger as he speaks.)

Cleopas: Here is the village where we live. Just in time, for it is getting dark.

Nathaniel: Sir, please do not go on alone. Stay with us and share our house and table.

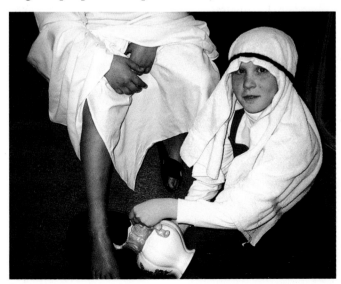

Jesus: Thank you. May God's blessing be upon you and your house.

Scene 4: The home of Cleopas and Nathaniel

Cleopas: Peace and welcome to our humble house.

Nathaniel: Permit me, Sir, to wash your feet. Come and join us at our table.

Stranger: Blessed be God.

Miriam: *(lights the candles and prays)* Our God and God of our Fathers and Mothers, bless our home with the light of your Spirit.

Cleopas: *(begins the prayer over the cup)* Praised be you, O Lord Our God. We raise our cups to sanctify your name.

Stranger: *(takes the bread, breaks it)* Take and eat this. It is my body, given for you.

(stranger fades stage rear)

Nathaniel: *(staring at the bread and at Cleopas)* It is the Lord Jesus!

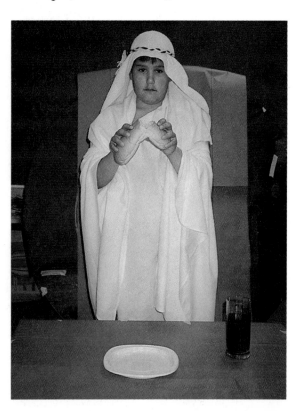

Remember the way he used to break bread with us.

Cleopas: It is him! Jesus is alive! Alleluia!

Nathaniel: No wonder our hearts were burning with excitement when he talked with us on the road. He explained the Scriptures just as Jesus did.

Cleopas: Nathaniel, we must go back. We must tell the others.

Nathaniel: Let's go.

Scene 5: In the upper room

(Cleopas and Nathaniel enter, excited)

James: *(to Cleopas and Nathaniel)* It is true. The Lord is risen!

Andrew: Yes. It is true! He has appeared to Nathaniel.

(women enter)

Mary Magdalene: It is true. We've been to the tomb.

Mary: He is risen!

Joanna: His tomb is empty.

Cleopas: *(excitedly blurts out)* You wouldn't believe what happened to us today. It was the most wonderful thing. Jesus walked with us. He talked with us. Would you believe it? It was not until he broke the bread, blessed it and gave it to us that we recognized him.

Nathaniel: Our hearts were burning within us as he talked to us on the road. It is true. We have seen the Lord.

Jesus: *(enters from the side)* Peace be with you!
(all step back in fright)

Jesus: Don't be afraid, my friends. Don't doubt. Yes, it is I. Touch me, if you find it hard to believe.

Peter: Is it really you, Lord?

Jesus: Yes, it is really I.

(The whole cast spreads out, joins hands in a circle and sings "In the Spirit We Live," No. 4.)

How did the two disciples come to recognize Jesus as their risen Lord?

What do you think Luke meant when he said "their eyes were opened"?

What do you think he meant when he said "they recognized him"?

Use this sequence of events to illustrate the story of Emmaus in your treasure book.

i)   The disciples share their experience of sadness.

ii) Jesus joins them on their way, sharing their sadness.

iii) He asks questions, discusses with them, refreshes their memory.

iv) He helps them understand what had happened, that Jesus had to suffer in order to enter into glory.

v)   The disciples invite Jesus to stay with them.

vi) Jesus breaks the bread and they recognize him.

vii) Excited, they go to the other disciples to share their story.

Remember

"...They told what had happened on the road, and how he had been made known to them in the breaking of the bread." (Luke 24.35)

8 We celebrate the breaking of the bread

Identify what is happening in each picture on these two pages. Arrange the events in their proper order to show the flow of a eucharistic celebration.

Design a stained glass window with similar illustrations to tell this story.

Breadmaking

Go back to your stained glass window. Find the panel where bread is being used. How is it used? Think for a moment. Why is bread so important in eucharistic celebrations?

Have you ever wondered how bread for eucharistic celebrations is made? Who bakes the bread? What ingredients are used? Get together with your friends and discuss these recipes before putting them to use.

Eucharistic bread

Preheat oven to 175°C (350°F).

625 mL (2 ½ cups) whole wheat flour
125 mL (½ cup) unbleached white flour
300 mL (1 ¼ cups) lukewarm water

Mix all the ingredients together in a bowl until all the flour is gathered together. Place the dough on the counter or bread board and knead for about 5 to 6 minutes. The dough is stiff, so very little extra flour will be necessary.

Kneading is most important to prevent puffing in the dough.

After the kneading, when the dough is smooth and pliable, form it into a ball and let it rest for about 5 minutes. Cover it with a damp cloth to prevent a crust from forming.

Sprinkle a little flour on the counter or bread board. Roll the dough until it is about 20 cm (8 inches) in diameter and about 6 mm (¼ inch) thick. Place the circles on a greased cookie sheet and score the dough with a knife.*

Bake the bread immediately after rolling. Bake for about 16 to 17 minutes. The bread should not brown, so the colour will remain pretty much the same but will lighten somewhat. It must not be overbaked, as some moisture is needed for the bread to have the proper texture.

Cool and wrap the bread in plastic or foil. Freeze it until a few hours before you use it.

Normally 125 to 140 portions can be obtained from one 20-cm (8-inch) round. This recipe makes two 20-cm (8-inch) rounds.

Unleavened bread

Preheat oven to 175°C (350°F).

1L (4 cups) whole wheat flour
500 mL (2 cups) warm water

Place water in bowl and gradually add whole wheat flour. Add an additional 125 mL to 250 mL (½ to 1 cup) whole wheat flour as needed to make dough stiff. (Additional flour should be added very slowly as the dough becomes stiff rapidly with kneading.)

Sprinkle a little flour on the counter or bread board. Roll out the dough until it is 12 mm (½ inch) thick, then cut it into two 25- to 30-cm (10- to 12-inch) circles or four 15-cm (6-inch) circles. Place the circles on a greased cookie sheet and score the dough with a knife.*

Bake the bread for about 16 to 17 minutes.

Remember

A eucharistic celebration has two main parts: the Liturgy of the Word and the Liturgy of the Eucharist. There are also introductory and concluding rites.

After it has baked, let it cool and then wrap it in plastic.

Prepare two separate batches of dough. Do not double the recipe: Make one batch of large circles and one batch of small circles.

* Scoring the bread

In preparing the bread for the Eucharist, it is important that the loaves be scored with a knife before baking. This will make it easier for the bread to be broken during the liturgy.

To score a circular loaf, press an open end of a glass in the centre, pressing it into, but not all the way through, the dough. Then, with a dull knife, trace concentric circles around the circle made by the glass. Then trace a cross in the centre circle and further score the loaf, with knife lines coming like spokes from the centre circle.

How are the two recipes different? How are they similar? How do they compare to other bread recipes?

What does the word *unleavened* mean?

Who provides eucharistic bread for your parish celebrations? Does someone in your community bake it?

Why do we call the celebration of the Eucharist "the breaking of the bread"?

9 We give praise and thanks to God

Pictures tell stories

What is happening in these pictures?
If someone asked you to draw a picture of your celebration, what would you draw? How would you describe the experience?

Write a story in your treasure book about how we live out the Eucharist.

Inside a Byzantine Church

A church building in the Byzantine tradition is like a family album. It is a place of gathering that reveals something about the people who are present. It also helps us to understand what is happening when the Church gathers to celebrate the Eucharist.

When you enter a Byzantine church, you get the impression that you have come into the presence of the sacred. Imagine that you are there for Sunday worship. Be one with the people who are gathering. Here is the gathering of the family of God in Christ!

Meet the family. Up high on the walls are icons of the **patriarchs** and prophets. They spoke about the coming of Christ and prepared people for it. Look at the images of the apostles, martyrs and saints. They are living witnesses of fidelity to Christ. We stand in their presence. We look to them for hope and inspiration. We pray to them and they pray with and for us. On the ceiling and the walls are many scenes from the story of redemption. It is not a story of something distant. It is our story, a story for now.

The **icon** of Mary, the Mother of God, stands in a very prominent place. She is the link between God and people. She is here praying with us and for us.

Stand in the centre of the building and look up. In the highest part of the church, the dome, is the icon of Christ the ruler, creator, the **Pantocrator**. He is the head of the gathering of the entire Church, the Church of heaven and the Church of earth. This is a great family feast. Christ gathers the whole Church into one great act of thanksgiving: the Eucharist.

Christic the Pantocrator

Look carefully at the icon of Christ the Pantocrator and discover a treasure of meaning!

Look at Christ's facial expression. What does it show?

Why is Christ's right hand raised? What does he hold in his left hand? Why?

Look at the three letters in the nimbus, that bright disk that surrounds Christ's head. What shape do they take? What do you think the letters mean?

new words

icon: from the Greek word *eikon,* meaning "image" or "likeness"

patriarchs: the founding fathers of our faith: Abraham, Isaac and Jacob

Pantocrator: ruler of all

Remember

"This is my body which will be given for you.... This cup is the new covenant in my blood which will be poured out for you." (Luke 22.19-20)

Unit 4
The Church expects the coming of the Lord

Theme 10 God will prepare a banquet for all people
Theme 11 Mary leads us in hope
Theme 12 We celebrate the promise

10 God will prepare a banquet for all people

Melissa's hope

Melissa tossed and turned, twisted and curled under her grandmother's warm, cozy quilt. It was way past her sleeping time, but Melissa was wide awake. A world of colour kept dancing around in her head. There were the new red mittens with stockings to match for five-year-old David, the soft pink nighties for babies Michelle and Margo, and the shiny silver desk set for Daniel Joseph. She could see it all as clear as day. Most of all, she could see the big, bright smiles of the Brandon family as they happily prepared their special Christmas Day feast. It was well into the night before Melissa drifted off to sleep.

Next morning, warm yellow light streamed into Melissa's room. Like a flash, her feet were on the floor.

Downstairs, Mom got out of her way. Melissa was like a bee in the kitchen. Finally, it was time to go to school. She ran upstairs to get the gift. Melissa's heart was glowing.

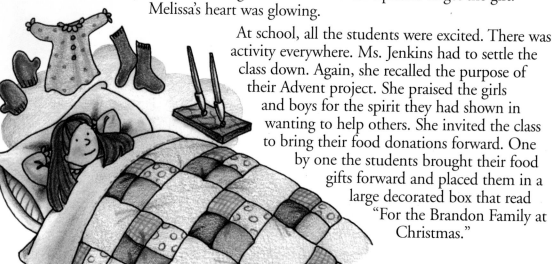

At school, all the students were excited. There was activity everywhere. Ms. Jenkins had to settle the class down. Again, she recalled the purpose of their Advent project. She praised the girls and boys for the spirit they had shown in wanting to help others. She invited the class to bring their food donations forward. One by one the students brought their food gifts forward and placed them in a large decorated box that read "For the Brandon Family at Christmas."

66

Jenny brought cranberry sauce to go with the turkey the school had contributed. Mary said her mom had baked a special cake and they had decorated it together. Billy said his grandmother helped him buy preserves in the market.

Melissa waited expectantly. Soon, it was her turn. Her donation was different. It was wrapped in shiny gold paper with the biggest, reddest bow. The students looked puzzled as Melissa came forward to place her gift in the box. From the beginning of the project they had noticed Melissa's excitement. Now they were even more curious. One thing was very clear. Melissa was happy.

"This project is very important to me." Melissa spoke softly. "Since Ms. Jenkins announced it, I have saved all the money that I could." The whole class was silent. Something in Melissa's voice made them take special notice. "I want to make the Brandon family extra happy," she continued, as she looked around the room at all the boys and girls. There was a long pause before Melissa spoke again. "You see, last Christmas my family received a Christmas box from a class just like ours. My dad was out of work and we had very little money. Christmas was looking sad at our house. On Christmas Eve, we received a visit from a class who brought us a hamper of food and gifts. I will never forget it. My mom was so happy she cried.

"We had a special prayer in our home that evening. Dad thanked God for all the people in the world who help others. He said we should always help our neighbours, especially at Christmas. He had a special hope. It was that each Christmas our family would make someone as happy as we were that night." Melissa stopped for a while. Slowly she continued, "This Christmas I have a special hope. I want to make the Brandon family as happy as we were."

Even Ms. Jenkins was quiet. Softly she invited the class to pray with her. After the prayer she shared a wonderful idea. "Remember when we agreed to select four representatives to come with me to deliver the hamper? Let's make Melissa one of these."

Hands shot up happily all around the room. Even Billy Evans shouted, "Right on! Let's have Melissa present the gift box, too." The students all agreed. Melissa's heart was afire. It sparkled in her eyes.

Why was Melissa so eager to make the family happy?

Is the title of the story a good one? What was Melissa's hope?

Why did the class choose this time of year to do this project?

Advent is here!

At this time we are waiting for Christmas to come. This liturgical season is called Advent. Advent is a time filled with anticipation and expectation. The word "advent" means "coming": it is a time of waiting, knowing that something important is about to happen. The one we expect and wait for in life is God. God is the food and the desire of people. During Advent we live out this deep hunger for God. We know God's answer to our hope: the Lord Jesus, God's greatest gift to the world. Each year we hope again that Jesus will lead us to God and will satisfy our hunger and thirst for light.

Weaving a basket of hope

Hi! My name is Sharon Breckenridge and I am a basket weaver from Thunder Bay, Ontario. I make all sorts of baskets, as you can see from this picture. I think baskets are wonderful – they're so lovely to look at and can hold all sorts of things: mitts and scarves, pencils, laundry, dried flowers, fruits and vegetables, and lots more.

When my son was in elementary school they had a large basket in the lunch room. If you were full and had something left over from your lunch, or if your mom or dad gave you something you didn't like, you could put it in the basket for someone else to share. Or, if you were extra hungry one day or forgot your lunch, you could take something from the basket. That's a really good way to use a basket, I think.

I understand you're going to make a basket together for your classroom. What a great idea! Each person in your class could bring something from home to weave into it and then it would be a basket that truly tells a story of all of you. And if you haven't anything at home, there are probably lots of things right in your classroom that you can use. Here are some suggestions: wool (single, double or even triple strands), strips of leather, raffia, bulrush leaves, paper twist, ribbon, rope, or string (doubled or tripled – even dyed).

I hope you have lots of fun with it. Happy weaving!

 Together with your friends, weave a basket and fill it with your hopes.

Prepare ye the way of the Lord!

A parish trims a mitten tree for families who need them. Does your community have an Advent tree? What do you call it? Why?

A family prepares a hamper for the needy. How does your community provide food for the needy?

During a Sunday liturgy, Isaiah's message is being proclaimed. What liturgical readings do you hear during Advent? Why?

Advent wreath candles are lit during a parish celebration. Do you have an Advent wreath at school? in your parish church?

A Christmas dinner is prepared for homeless people. How does your community reach out to the homeless?

How does the title of this page link with the drawings?

Do you know where the title comes from?

What signs of Advent and hope do you see in your parish?

70

Make his paths straight

John's origins
    Luke 1.5-25;
    36-37; 39; 44;
    56-80

His preaching
    Luke 3.1-18
    Matthew 3.1-12
    Mark 1.1-6
    John 1.15; 19-28

His pointing out and
baptizing Jesus
    Matthew 3.13-17
    Mark 1.9-11
    John 1.29-34

Design a triptych to go along with your research. Show John baptizing Jesus on the centre panel.

The Advent wreath is round, with no beginning and no end, just like God's love.

The wreath is made of evergreen branches, which stay green even in winter and remind us of the gift of life.

The wreath has four candles – one for each week of Advent. As we light one more candle each week, we can see how we are getting closer to celebrating Jesus' coming.

W̲e remember and celebrate the hope of God's promise, Isaiah who spoke it, and the people of God who waited for the fulfilment of God's promise.

Blessing of the wreath

O God of all ages,
We praise you for Jesus Christ,
the hope of all peoples.
Let your blessing come upon us
as we gather in his name,
and bless this wreath
as we await the coming of our Lord.
We ask this through Jesus Christ, our Lord.

Closing prayer

O God of all ages,
you utter a word of promise and hope.
For you we wait; for you we listen.
Keep us alert.
Make us attentive to your word.
Grant this through him whose coming is certain
whose day draws near:
your Son, our Lord Jesus Christ,
who lives and reigns with you in the unity of the Holy Spirit,
God forever and ever.

[words and phrases adapted from the first and fourth Sundays of Advent, Years C and B in *Sunday Celebration of the Word and Hours*]

How are you and your friends making Advent come alive?

Remember

"Look, the young woman is with child and shall bear a son, and shall name him Immanuel."
(Isaiah 7.14)

11 Mary leads us in hope

"Your twins have arrived!"

The letter arrived on July 10th. It had a Colombian stamp. I opened it with my heart in my mouth. It announced, quite simply, "Your twins have arrived."

I was both stunned and overjoyed. For so long, Bert and I had been trying to adopt a baby. We had nearly given up hope: the obstacles seemed too great. And here was a letter telling us we had two babies waiting for us in Bogota, Colombia – a boy and a girl.

The next three weeks were quite crazy. I still had two weeks to teach in school. My class found me totally distracted, until I decided to share my excitement with them. They were over the moon with me.

Meanwhile, my head was full of plans. We needed two cribs, two low chairs, two feeding bottles, two sets of everything. How could we get the nursery ready in time? What baby clothes would we take with us to Colombia? And what were we going to call the babies?

I went into school one day and told my class that we had just heard the children's names: Pedro and Blanca. I told them

Bert and I thought they really needed English names, and we had chosen Benjamin and Rebecca. The whole class erupted. "No, no," they insisted, "they must always be Pedro and Blanca." So that was decided.

As the day for our journey halfway across the world drew nearer, we checked and rechecked our papers. Everything seemed in order: the medical papers, the birth and marriage certificates, the bank statements, the adoption forms, the official notary's stamp of approval. The papers probably weighed more than the babies did!

Family, friends and neighbours kept calling with gifts: a baby bath, blankets, teddy bears and piles of diapers. My class made two enormous soft toys and a mobile for the nursery. I was in a state of unspeakable excitement. I spent hours shopping, savouring the joy of choosing baby clothes, bathtime soaps and oils.

On August 2nd we flew to Bogota. It was almost unreal, travelling for 16 hours in order to reach the babies who were to make our family complete. The final hours of waiting seemed the longest of all. When we arrived at the convent, the babies were not there. They were at the clinic. We were told to go and have a much-needed siesta.

They woke us half an hour later to usher us into the parlour. Twenty nuns lined the walls to see our reaction. Then the door opened, and our babies were brought in. The little boy was wrapped in a blue blanket, the little girl in yellow. All we could see were tiny fists, black hair, and two enormous pairs of shining black eyes.

I took the smaller of the two bundles into my arms, and Bert took Blanca into his. A tiny hand shot out, plucked his sunglasses from his shirt pocket, and dropped them onto the floor. "That's my girl," he said. I hugged my little blue bundle, and hoped that the love I felt for Pedro and his sister would reach his heart.

Have you ever had the experience of longing and hoping for someone or something? Have you ever waited for the arrival of a brother or sister?

Get together with your friends and share your experiences.

I am the handmaid of the Lord

The Annunciation

In the sixth month, the angel Gabriel was sent by God to a town in Galilee called Nazareth, to a virgin betrothed to a man named Joseph, of the House of David; and the virgin's name was Mary. He went in and said to her, "Greetings, favoured one! The Lord is with you." She was deeply disturbed by these words and asked herself what this greeting could mean, but the angel said to her, "Do not be afraid, Mary, for you have found favour with God. Listen! You are to conceive and bear a son, and you must name him Jesus. He will be great and will be called Son of the Most High. The Lord God will give him the throne of his ancestor David; he will reign over the House of Jacob for ever and his kingdom will have no end." Mary said to the angel, "But how can this come about, since I am a virgin?" "The Holy Spirit will come upon you," the angel answered, "and the power of the Most High will cover you with its shadow. And so the child will be holy and will be called Son of God. Know this too: your kinswoman Elizabeth has, in her old age, herself conceived a son, and she whom people called barren is now in her sixth month, for nothing is impossible to God." "I am the handmaid of the Lord," said Mary. "Let what you have said be done to me." And the angel left her. (See Luke 1.26-38.)

What was Mary's reaction to the greeting of the angel?

What was the angel's response?

When Mary had listened to the angel's message, what was her first response?

What were the angel's final words to Mary? What was Mary's response?

How is this a story of hope?

Read Luke 1.39-45 to find out what Mary did after she heard the angel's message.

The Magnificat is Mary's song of praise and thanksgiving. It is one of the best known Christian songs. It is sung by those who pray the Church's evening prayer. Design a prayer plaque for your home with the words of the Magnificat.

The Magnificat

And Mary said:

"My soul magnifies the Lord,
and my spirit rejoices in God my Saviour,
for he has looked with favour on the lowliness of his servant.
Surely, from now on all generations will call me blessed;
for the Mighty One has done great things for me,
and holy is his name.
His mercy is for those who fear him from generation to generation.
He has shown strength with his arm;
he has scattered the proud in the thoughts of their hearts.
He has brought down the powerful from their thrones,
and lifted up the lowly;
he has filled the hungry with good things, and sent the rich away empty.
He has helped his servant Israel, in remembrance of his mercy,
according to the promise he made to our ancestors,
to Abraham and to his descendants forever."
(Luke 1.46-55)

For what does Mary praise God?

Why is Mary so happy?

What does Mary sing about?

Join with Mary and the Church in singing the Magnificat.

Remember

Mary is the mother of the Messiah.

12 We celebrate the promise

Jesse was a shepherd who lived in Bethlehem about 1000 years before Jesus. One day, God sent the prophet Samuel to Bethlehem to choose and anoint one of Jesse's sons to be King of Israel. Jesse brought each of his seven sons to Samuel. They were tall and handsome and strong-looking. Samuel was sure that God would want him to choose one of them. But no, God told him to ask Jesse if he had any more sons. Jesse was surprised. "Yes," he answered, "my youngest son, David, is out in the field looking after the sheep."

Painting the Jesse Tree symbols

Samuel told Jesse to send for David. And right away, the prophet knew that this young boy was God's choice. Taking the horn of oil, Samuel anointed David right

there where he stood with his brothers. The Bible story tells us that "God's Spirit came to David and stayed with him from that day on."*

And that is why, during Advent, Christians make Jesse Trees. They helps us remember the story of David and all the other important people who were part of Jesus' story. The Jesse Tree is something like Jesus' family tree.

* (Adapted from 1 Samuel 16.1-13.)

Eternal God,
in the psalms of David,
in the words of the prophets,
in the dream of Joseph
your promise is spoken.

At last, in the womb of the Virgin Mary,
your Word takes flesh.
Teach us to welcome Jesus, the promised Emmanuel,
and to preach the good news of his coming,
that every age may know him
as the source of love and life.

A stone of hope

Decorating the Jesse Tree

Grant this through him whose
coming is certain,
whose day draws near:
your Son, our Lord Jesus Christ,
who lives and reigns with you in
the unity of the Holy Spirit,
God forever and ever. Amen.

[from the opening prayer for the
Fourth Sunday of Advent,
Sunday Celebration of the Word and Hours]

Prepare your own Advent celebration and decorate your Jesse Tree.

Meet Advent joy-bringers!

Hi! My name is Khristina Zayac. As a white face clown, I love to lead others in movements and gestures. Sometimes I get into a mischievous mood and do funny things, like tying another clown's shoelaces together to trip them. I don't ever hurt anyone, though. I only play tricks like throwing water on another clown's head if I've asked for permission to do so first. My favourite prop is a flower that squirts water when someone tries to smell it.

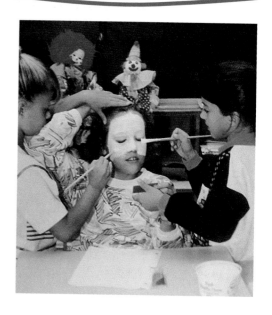

I'm Frances Ricci, an Auguste clown. I sure am clumsy. Everything seems to happen to me! Often I trip over my shoelaces and end up sprawled across the floor. I think people laugh with me, because sometimes they do silly things without even trying. I help them feel better about those times. At times I exaggerate and do things that really can't work, like trying to ride a bike that has square wheels.

My name is Shawn Lagace, a real tramp. I'm often down and out, but I don't mind because the people I meet are very caring and kind towards me. My clothes are baggy and worn. The children I meet often try to make me smile and feel better about myself. I think that brings them a lot of warmth, too. They end up with a welcome look on their faces.

Hello there! I'm Aaron Borgatti. Garfield has always been my favourite cartoon character, so it wasn't difficult for me to decide who I wanted to look like. I used orange and black to help me look like a cat. Just like Garfield, I love to act silly and make people laugh. However, I try not to be quite as sarcastic as Garfield, because sometimes people don't quite understand and their feelings get hurt. That's what a clown tries never to do!

Take some quiet time to discover the clown who is inside you!
What's your favourite clown?
Do you have a choice of costume?
What kind of clown would you like to be?
Do you have a favourite clown name?

Everyone has a clown inside!

Clowns give without expecting anything in return, except laughter, a smile, joy to break our sadness. Clowns take risks but they are not afraid, because they know the real joy of life. They are like David when the Israelites brought the Ark of the Covenant to Jerusalem. David was so happy that he "leaped and danced before God." He said, "I am willing to act like a fool in order to show my joy in the Lord." (2 Samuel 6.16-21)

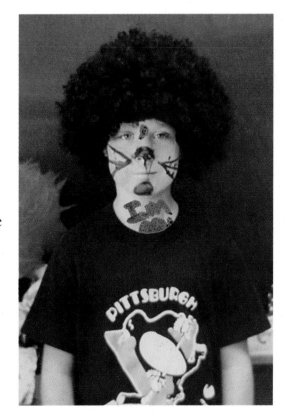

A clown's prayer

Creator God,
We thank you for the gift of
    laughter.
We thank you for the gift of
    your Spirit,
giving us energy to go out
    and share with others.
May our laughter bring
    healing and joy
to us and those we touch.
May we respect and honour
    your presence
in everyone we meet.
This we ask through Christ
    our Lord.
Amen.

new words

ark of the covenant:
a Hebrew religious object
in the form of a portable
shrine containing the two
tablets of the law. It was a
symbol of God's presence
in Israel. Also referred to as
the Ark of God.

Remember
Advent is a season of hope.

Unit 5
The Church welcomes all the nations

Theme 13 God chooses a people
Theme 14 God is faithful
Theme 15 The Lord welcomes all the nations

13 God chooses a people

"Arise, shine out, for your light has come,
the glory of the Lord is rising on you...
The nations come to your light
and kings to your dawning brightness."

(See Isaiah 60.1-3.)

The visit of the Magi

The Church proclaims these words at the feast of Epiphany. Do you know why? What does this passage refer to? What does the word *epiphany* mean?

Discover all you can about the feast of Epiphany. Begin by reading the story of the magi in Matthew 2.1-12. In your treasure book, describe how the story tells us about God's welcoming all people.

Look again at Isaiah's message on the opposite page. Why does the Church use Isaiah's image of a star's shining light? What does a star do?

In addition to the story of the magi, we hear two other stories during the feast of Epiphany. See the art on this page. Why these stories?

Design a star to hang in your home as a reminder of Epiphany. Write these or similar words on it: "May this star be a sign that God loves us and all people."

The Wedding Feast at Cana

Jesus' baptism in the Jordan

During the feast of Epiphany, we celebrate how God seeks out all people. It is a celebration of God's welcoming all nations. It is a celebration of God's love for us, of God's promise to us.

 Have you ever thought about how we reflect this promise in our everyday relationships with people? Read the story of promise below. What word best describes this family relationship?

My story of promise

One day ago, I promised my mother that I would love her for the rest of my life and in return my mother promised the same thing. I felt very happy when my mother said," I'll love you for the rest of your life" I always pray that nobody will ever break my promise with my mother, nobody!

Avril Michelle Weber

Lord, I pray that my mom and I never break our promise because that promise means everything to me!

 Write your own promise prayer in your treasure book.

Covenant stones

The texts from the Bible reflect a special agreement or *covenant* between God and people.

Covenants are treaties or agreements between people or nations. In a covenant, one person or nation promises to protect another in return for certain commitments.

When God makes a covenant, it is like an adoption. God makes the first move toward people, particularly people who can no longer help themselves. Out of pure love and friendship, God offers to come to their help and adopt them as God's own.

Read the covenant words printed on the stones below. What do they tell us about God's covenant?

Draw your own collection of covenant stones in your treasure book. Share them with your friends and family.

AND KNOW THAT I AM WITH YOU ALWAYS; YES, TO THE END OF TIME.
(See Matthew 28.20.)

WITH YOU I WILL MAKE AN EVERLASTING COVENANT.
(See Isaiah 55.3.)

I HAVE LOVED YOU WITH AN EVERLASTING LOVE; I WILL ALWAYS LOVE YOU.
(See Jeremiah 31.3.)

I HAVE CALLED YOU BY NAME, YOU ARE MINE.
(See Isaiah 43.1.)

I WILL BE YOUR GOD AND YOU WILL BE MY PEOPLE.
(See Ezekiel 37.28.)

God's covenant story begins

The Joy of God's promise

Abram and Sarai lived a long time ago. First they lived at Ur; then they moved to a place called Haran. Because they had herds of animals, Abram and Sarai sometimes had to move all of their possessions great distances in order to find good pasture land.

Once, when Abram was coming to Canaan, God spoke to him. God told Abram that one day all of this land would belong to his children, grandchildren and great grandchildren. Abram did not question the promise of God, even though he and Sarai had no children. Instead he built an altar as a sign of his faithfulness and prayed to God.

Later, when Abram had moved his herds farther into Canaan, God again promised him that this land would one day belong to his descendants. This time Abram questioned the promise of God, saying, "See, you have given me no descendants; some man of my household will be my heir."

God answered, "Your heir shall be of your own flesh and blood." To illustrate the promise, God told Abram to go outside his tent and count the stars in the night sky. Then God said to Abram, "Such will be your descendants."

As time went on, Abram

became a very old man. Still he and Sarai did not have children. One day God came to him and said, "Here now is my covenant with you: you shall become the father of a multitude of nations. You shall no longer be called Abram; your name shall be Abraham, for I make you father of a multitude of nations. I will make you most fruitful. I will establish my covenant between myself and you, and your descendants after you, generation after generation, an everlasting covenant, and I will be your God." The name which God gave Abraham means "the father exalted." God went on to say to Abraham, "As for Sarai your wife, you shall not call her Sarai but Sarah. I will bless her and give you a son by her." Abraham bowed to the ground. He thought to himself, "Is a child to be born to a man 100 years old, and will Sarah have a child at the age of 90?" The name which God gave Sarah means "princess." Although Abraham did not understand all he had been promised, he did not lose faith.

Several years later, three visitors came to the tent of Abraham and Sarah to ask for food. Abraham commanded his servants to bring them bread, cheese and milk. One of the visitors asked for Sarah. Abraham told them that she was in the tent. The visitor promised to return in the spring when Sarah had a son. Sarah, who was listening, laughed aloud when she heard his forecast.

Strange as it may seem, the promise of God began to unfold and Sarah gave birth to Isaac, whose name means "laughing."

 Find the covenant words in the story and write them on stones in your treasure book.

God's covenant story continues with Moses

Moses is a great hero in the Book of Exodus in the Bible. It was Moses to whom God gave the dangerous task of leading the people out of Egypt to the freedom of a new home. Moses cried out to God, "Please send somebody else!" But God assured him, "Trust me, Moses. I will be with you."

 Read the following scripture texts to learn more about God's covenant with Moses:

Exodus 2.1-10
Exodus 2.11-24
Exodus 3.1-15
Exodus 15.1-19
Exodus 15.20
Exodus 19.1-9
Exodus 20.1-17
Exodus 24.1-8
Exodus 25.1-22

With your friends, design an ark of the covenant for your prayer centre. Read Exodus 25.10-22 to see how the ark was made. What will you put in the ark? Why?

On eagle's wings

Have you ever observed an eagle teaching its young to fly? Can you imagine what happens?

From a nest high in the mountains, the mother eagle, with her young on her back, flies straight into the air! Gently, she lets go of her young. Imagine the young eagle stretching its wings to fly!

When the wind is too strong, the mother eagle is there to break the fall. She swoops down to save her young from falling. Catching it once again on her back, the mother eagle continues to teach her little one until it learns to ride the wind. How exciting it is to finally see the young eagle streak through the sky!

Why do you think the Bible uses the image of an eagle to show how God cares for us?

In your treasure book, draw your own image of how God cares for us.

new words

covenant: the bond that binds God to us and us to God

epiphany: manifestation, revealing, making apparent

Remember

"I will be your God and you will be my people." (See Ezekiel 37.28.)

14 God is faithful

Ruth and Naomi

This story begins with a famine in the land of Judah. For months there was no rain. Nothing would grow, and so people were starving.

"We must go to another country until there is rain," said Elimelech to his wife, Naomi. And so they took their two sons and everything they owned and started on their journey to the land of Moab. There they settled. But not long after, Naomi's husband died. Her two sons grew up and married young Moabite women, Orpah and Ruth, who came to live with their husbands in Naomi's home. They loved their mother-in-law, Naomi. And Naomi loved and welcomed Orpah and Ruth into her home.

About ten years later, Naomi's two sons died and Naomi was left without husband or sons. She was sad. But then she heard that there was bread again in Judah and she decided to return home. She said to her daughters-in-law, "I am going back to live with my own people." But Ruth and Orpah would not let her go alone. They went along with her on the journey back to Judah.

When they came to the border, Naomi turned to them and said, "Go back, my daughters. Return to your mother's house. Stay in your own country where you will find husbands again. I will not be able to care for you. May God be kind to you because you have been kind to me."

Weeping, Orpah kissed Naomi goodbye and went back to her home. But Ruth loved Naomi very much and would not leave her. She insisted on continuing the journey. These are her words to Naomi:

"Wherever you go, I will go, wherever you live, I will live. Your people shall be my people, and your God, my God." (See Ruth 1.16.)

Naomi saw that Ruth was determined to go with her, so she said no more. The two women travelled on to Naomi's old home in Bethlehem. When they arrived there, they saw the fields rich in grain, ripe for the harvest.

But Naomi and Ruth were very poor. They had no money to buy food. So God took care of them in another way. According to Jewish law, widows and poor people could harvest in the corners of the field. It was very hard work and often Ruth's heart was sad as she gathered the sheaves. Every morning she went out, and in the evening she brought the grain back to Naomi. With this they were able to make bread.

Now the owner of the field was a wealthy man named Boaz. One day when he was walking out to see the harvest, he noticed Ruth. Calling his servant, Boaz asked about her. The servant told him that she was a Gentile from Moab and praised her for her kindness to her mother-in-law, Naomi.

Boaz was a good man. He was very touched by Ruth's loyalty. He told her she was welcome to take grain from his fields and to share the food and drink of his own people. He said to her:

"May the Lord reward you for your deeds, and may you have a full reward from the Lord, the God of Israel, under whose wings you have come for refuge!" (Ruth 2.12)

That evening, Naomi was surprised to see how much grain Ruth had collected. Then Ruth told her how kind Boaz had been. Imagine Ruth's surprise when Naomi told her that Boaz was a relative. According to Jewish custom, Boaz was encouraged to marry the young widow Ruth. And soon after, Ruth gave birth to a son, Obed. Obed was the father of Jesse, who was the father of David.

Each year at harvest time, Jews remember this beautiful story. Can you guess why?

How does the story reflect God's faithfulness?

How does it reflect God's welcoming?

How is it a story of belonging?

Read Ruth 1.16 once more. Write the words in your Big Treasure Book.

Jonah and the great fish

One day God spoke to Jonah. "Jonah, I want you to go to the people of Nineveh and tell them that if they don't get their act together, the city will be blown apart!"

Jonah listened politely but thought, "No way, God. I don't like those Ninevites one bit. You are our God and not God of the Ninevites." Jonah tried to think of a place where he could get away from God. He went down to the port of Joppa to board a ship for Tarshish, which was in the opposite direction from Nineveh. The thought of getting away from God pleased Jonah very much, for God's requests were too hard.

While they were out at sea, they ran into a bad storm. The sea was splashing up on board and the ship was rocking fiercely. In their fright, the sailors prayed to their gods, hoping to live through the storm.

But where was Jonah?

In the raging storm, the captain went to find him and saw him sleeping. The captain shook Jonah awake. "What is the matter with you? Is this any time to sleep? Get up and start praying! For all I know, this could be the last hour of your life! Tell your God to come and help us, because God is our only hope now."

Meanwhile, the sailors were talking among themselves trying to figure out who was to blame for this bad luck. One sailor piped up, "It's Jonah! From the moment I saw him, I knew he would be trouble."

So they all scrambled down to the deck, looking for Jonah. Once they found him, they questioned him: "Why did you board our ship? And where do you come from?"

"I'm a Hebrew," Jonah told them. "I'm running away from God because I refuse to do what God commands me to do."

"So you are the cause of our bad luck! How are we going to get out of this storm?" the sailors asked.

"Throw me overboard, and that will calm the storm," said Jonah.

The sailors were quite surprised that Jonah took the blame. The storm became stronger and stronger, and they all prayed to Jonah's God.

"O God," they prayed, "don't let us die if we throw this man overboard; don't hold it against us. The storm is your doing."

Finally, fear made them decide to throw Jonah overboard. They tossed him into the sea. As he hit the water, the storm calmed down right away. The sailors couldn't believe their eyes. They were so impressed by this show of power that they worshipped God.

God sent a great fish to swallow Jonah. Once Jonah had regained consciousness, he couldn't figure out where he was. He thought at first that he was in a big cave. Soon he figured out where he was and decided to pray.

In three days' time, the great fish burped up Jonah onto the shore so he could travel to Nineveh. Again God called to him. "Jonah, Jonah! You can see I am much more powerful than you, so you might as well give in. I will keep searching you out until you help me."

"All right, all right!" said Jonah. "But this is the last time I do a favour for you! Just look at me! There's seaweed in my hair and ears, and half of my clothes have been digested by that fish! How am I to expect anyone in Nineveh to listen to what I have to say if I look like this?"

God consoled Jonah and instructed him for a second time on what to say to the people of Nineveh. This time Jonah got up and went to Nineveh as God had asked.

Nineveh was a huge city. It took three days to walk from one end of it to the other. So Jonah spent a day walking and proclaiming to the people that they were in big trouble. "In forty days' time," he shouted, "this city will become a heap of garbage!"

As soon as the people of Nineveh heard this, they were horrified. Rich and poor turned from their evil ways. They put on sackcloth, fasted and prayed. Soon the news reached the king, who also stripped himself of his royal clothes, put on sackcloth and prayed. The king issued a proclamation to repent, and the messengers carried it throughout the city.

Touched by the response of the people, God did not destroy the city but blessed it instead.

Jonah grumbled once more about God's concern for the Ninevites. In exasperation God said to Jonah, "Why can't you accept that I feel sorry for the great city of Nineveh? These people deserve my mercy as much as you do!"

 Like the story of Ruth and Naomi, the story of Jonah also shows how God loves and welcomes people of all races and nations. Get together with your friends and present the story in an art form of your choice. Be sure it shows your viewers the key message.

A prayer of remembering

*God sees a world that knows no despair,
a vision of justice and love.
There is great joy for the people who share
God's covenant of promise and love.*

*We remember that God cares for Israel as
an eagle cares for its nestlings. God's care is
shown in the covenant with Israel.*

*We remember the covenant with Abraham
and Sarah: "I will give you a country; your
children will be as numerous as the stars in
the heavens."*

*We remember the covenant with Moses and
Miriam. God led the people out of slavery,
through the desert, into the promised land.*

*We remember the story of Ruth and Naomi,
who tells us that the promise of the
covenant is for everyone.*

*We remember Jonah's words to God: "I
knew you were a God of tenderness and
compassion, slow to anger, and rich in
mercy."*

*We remember the covenant God made with
us in Jesus. God's love shines out for us in
Jesus' life, death and resurrection. Let us
proclaim the mystery of our faith:*

> *Christ has died, Christ is risen,
> Christ will come again.*

*God of the covenant,
we stand before you on holy ground,
for your name is glorified
and your mercy revealed*

*whenever your mighty deeds are
remembered.**

*Save us from whatever leads away from you;
in your love, draw us back to Jesus Christ,
who gave himself up for the sake of all.***

*We ask this through our Lord Jesus Christ
who lives and reigns with you in the unity
of the Holy Spirit,
God for ever and ever.*

*[Year C, Third Sunday in Lent]
**[adapted, Year C, Fourth Sunday of Lent]

**Create your own prayer of
remembering to share at
home. Remember your family
and friends in your prayer.**

Remember

"Wherever you go, I will go,
wherever you live, I will live. Your
people shall be my people, and your
God, my God." (See Ruth 1.16.)

15 The Lord welcomes all the nations

The flame of faith!

Do you know the story of the Olympic torch?
Do you know where its journey begins?
Who carries the torch? Why? What is its destination?

Now think about the flame of faith that began its journey long ago in Jerusalem.

Do you remember how it began?
Who helped the early Church to grow?

Look at the world map on this page. A flame representing the spread of God's faithfulness to all nations is drawn on each continent. Using blackline masters that your teacher will give you, read the story of each flame and discover how faith was carried throughout the world. Remember the work of God's Spirit!

Sketch a world map for your classroom, adding a flame to each continent. Match the blackline masters with the continents and place them on the map.

Diversity in unity

Led by the Holy Spirit and faithful to Jesus' command to reach out to all nations, the apostles carried the good news to many parts of the world. Wherever they went, they tried to awaken people's faith in Christ and to encourage them to accept the gospel message.

The apostles first preached in Jerusalem, the birthplace of Christianity. Within a short time, the apostles took the message of Christ beyond Jerusalem, and Christianity came to life in many areas. In the East, Antioch and Alexandria were developed, cultural centres. Rome, the capital of the Roman Empire, was the most important cultural centre of the West. These four cities greatly influenced the development of the early Christian Church.

When communities accepted Christianity, they accepted the same faith that the apostles taught. However, groups from the large cultural centres responded to the gospel message in their own way. These developed their own worship, traditions and creed. The large centres influenced the smaller neighbouring communities, and the major rites of the Church came into existence.

Take a look at the rites on this page. These belong to the Eastern Catholic Churches.

Can you find the Eastern rite that you have been learning about this year?

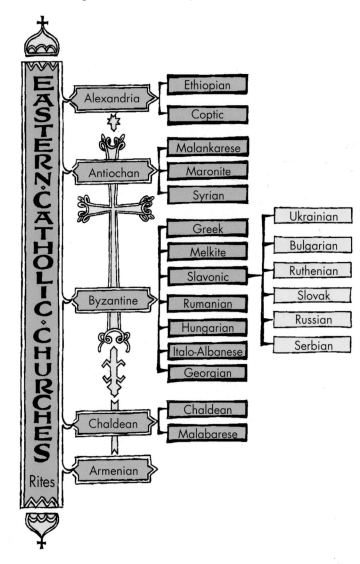

EASTERN CATHOLIC CHURCHES
Rites

- Alexandria
  - Ethiopian
  - Coptic
- Antiochan
  - Malankarese
  - Maronite
  - Syrian
- Byzantine
  - Greek
  - Melkite
  - Slavonic
    - Ukrainian
    - Bulgarian
    - Ruthenian
    - Slovak
    - Russian
    - Serbian
  - Rumanian
  - Hungarian
  - Italo-Albanese
  - Georgian
- Chaldean
  - Chaldean
  - Malabarese
- Armenian

Faith ignites in Canada!

Between the years 1600 and 1700, missionaries set out from Europe to go to a new land: Canada.

Can you imagine the journey in those days? Can you imagine what the new land was like – no roads, dense forest, no electricity! Why did these missionaries come?

What made these men and women take on such a challenge?

The missionaries' faith was strong. They were anxious to pass it on. They wanted to spread the good news. Led by the Spirit of Jesus, they soon dotted the shores of the St. Lawrence and beyond with little communities of Christians. For years before the official founding of dioceses in Canada, missionaries were at work spreading the faith. Churches were built. Christians gathered in little communities, giving witness to the presence of Jesus in their midst.

 Take some time to study a map or atlas of Canada. With your friends, make a representation of the map for your classroom wall. Print on the map the names of Canada's provinces and major cities. Then, use the dates given here for the official founding of dioceses in Canada to mark your map:

Diocese	Date founded	Diocese	Date founded
Quebec	1674	St. John's, NF	1847
Kingston	1826	St. Boniface	1847
Charlottetown	1829	Ottawa	1847
Montreal	1836	Hamilton	1856
Toronto	1841	London	1856
Halifax	1842	Grand Falls, NF	1856
Saint John, NB	1842	Edmonton	1871
Antigonish	1844	Regina	1910
Victoria	1846	Winnipeg	1915

Using flames as you did earlier, locate your own diocese on the map and mark it with a flame.

Research the story of your diocese, giving attention to early key witnesses of the faith. In particular, research the faith story of your parish. You might begin by contacting your Diocesan Office of Religious Education for information. Where possible, set up interviews with key witnesses of the faith.

Interview questions:

- Why did they come?
- When did they come?
- How did they come?
- How did they begin?
- What joys, growth, difficulties did they experience?
- What have they done and what are they doing in our parish or diocese?
- What are the results of their work in the Church?
- What evidence shows the action of the Spirit?

Children gather around Archbishop Peter Mallon in the Archdiocese of Regina.

When you have gathered all your information, plan an exhibit of the faith story of your parish and diocese.

A celebration of God's faithfulness to all nations

E ven though we come from different countries, reflect different races and speak different languages, the Holy Spirit of Jesus unites us in our celebration of one faith.

Opening Prayer

Ever-living God,
glory of those who believe in you,
fill the world with your splendor
and show every nation the radiance
of your light.
We ask this through our Lord Jesus
Christ, your Son,
who lives and reigns with you in the
unity of the Holy Spirit
God for ever and ever.

[from "The Second Sunday of Christmas" in
Sunday Celebration of the Word and Hours]

Remember

"You will receive power when the Holy Spirit has come upon you, and you will be my witnesses in Jerusalem, in all Judaea and Samaria, and to the ends of the earth." (See Acts 1.8.)

Unit 6
The Church acts justly

16 Anyone who welcomes you, welcomes me

A man of compassion

In the city of Hull, in the province of Quebec, lived a little man with a warm, friendly spirit. He would always go out for a morning walk and the children of the neighbourhood loved to tag along. They would talk about all sorts of things that interested them. He asked them about their families, what they were doing in school and what they intended to do when they grew up. He was always interested in their stories. Saturdays and holidays were special, because the children did not have to rush away to school.

One child remembers a time when he was new in the town. "Who is the little man you kids love to walk with?" his mom asked. Imagine her surprise when the child answered, "That's the bishop – Bishop Adolphe Proulx – our best friend on the block!"

Bishop Proulx tried to be everybody's friend. He loved the little people and those who were being mistreated. Like Jesus, the bishop tried to wake up those who were insensitive to others, insisted that we are all sisters and brothers and that we must share the good things of the earth, especially food, clothing and shelter.

On one occasion Bishop Proulx discovered that the government was about to close down a home for the elderly, without finding another place for these people. The bishop was angry and told the newspapers and the television and radio stations that if the government insisted on doing this, he would invite all these elderly people to come and live at his own house!

What do you think happened?

Research the work of Bishop Adolphe Proulx and find out what happened to the home for the elderly.
Discuss how Bishop Proulx stood for justice.

Design a scroll

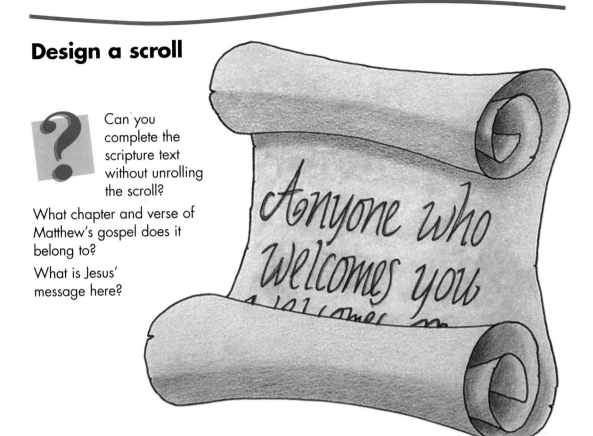

Can you complete the scripture text without unrolling the scroll?

What chapter and verse of Matthew's gospel does it belong to?

What is Jesus' message here?

Anyone who welcomes you

Look up the gospel references below to find out how Jesus cared for people. Choose your favourite text and design a similar scroll. Roll it up. Exchange scrolls with your friends.

- Luke 7.36-50
- Luke 14.12-14
- Luke 19.1-10

- Mark 2.1-12
- Mark 2.15-17
- Mark 3.1-6

Add the scrolls to your storytelling centre.

It's no game

Nirushan lives in Niagara Falls, Ontario. One day, Nirushan and his Grade 8 class played a game designed to illustrate how injustice exists in our world – how it feels to be poor while others have plenty. To Nirushan, the game was much more!

Nirushan is a recent immigrant to Canada. He came to Niagara Falls from Sri Lanka, a beautiful island country off the coast of India. However, Sri Lanka is a country with many poor people. Nirushan's people struggled hard to survive. He and his friends worked under difficult circumstances for little pay, often barely enough for a crust of bread. In such a beautiful and bountiful country, how could such poverty exist? Why would the wealth of the country be owned by a few?

As the game drew to a close, the students gathered to share their feelings. Nirushan gave a touching account: "You're fortunate that this experience is only a game," he said. "For my people in Sri Lanka, it's real. Every day they live this injustice." He ended with a strong message for his classmates and for us:

"Life is about love and trust and equality. In a world with so many gifts, no one should be hungry. We are all equal and should be treated with respect and dignity. This is your right. It is my right. It is the right of all people."

What challenge does this message present to our world today?

Write Nirushan's message and place it where all can see it.

What choice do we have?

Two farmers, each with a son and a daughter, go to centre stage. Government Officials, Food Company Representatives and Landlord wait in the wings.

Government Official *(enters)*: I am your representative from the government. There will be a meeting tonight of all the people on this land.

(Government Official leaves and returns with Food Company Representative and Landlord)

Government Official: Good evening. The government has a great plan for the land upon which you live. You farmers realize that your land could produce much more if you could use better machinery and control the weeds and insects through spraying. Tonight I have brought with me someone from the Food Company who has a marvellous idea.

Food Company Representative: We will help your country become more modern. What your country needs to become modern is money. Trade with rich countries pays you so you can buy all the good things of life. To help your country, we have decided to start a plantation here. The owner has sold us a lease to this land.

Farmers: But, for as long as we know, our families have lived here and worked the land for generations. Do we not have the rights to this land?

Landlord *(harshly)*: You own nothing here! I own this land. This piece of paper gives me a legal title to these 5000 hectares.

Government Official: By the beginning of next month you must leave this land. You will have to live over here. *(crowds the farmers and their sons and daughters into the small area)* Planting will start in three weeks.

Landlord: The Company will select some of you to work on the plantation. They will pay you workers $15.00 per week.

(A few farmers are picked out and led away from the others.)

1st Farmer's son: There is no work for me here anymore. I'll have to go to the city to find a job. They will need truck drivers and dockworkers to ship the produce. *(leaves)*

Farmer's daughters: Maybe some of the rich people in the city need someone to take care of their children. We'll send home some money whenever we can.

Narrator: It is now several years later. The small number of farmers left on the land have had a hard time. They were left very little land to grow their gardens. The little extra earning that the Company gave is hardly enough to keep the family alive.

2nd Farmer's son: They have brought new machines for harvesting the crops; I am no longer needed here. *(sits down)*

Government Official: Some people who do not like our program of helping people have formed a terrorist group. We need soldiers in our army. We will pay you $20.00 a week and we will give you all the food and clothing you need. Come and join us!

2nd Farmer's son: What choice do I have? I need a job to live. I need a job. *(leaves)*

Talk about the play in light of justice.

What would you do in this situation if you were a farmer? a government official? a food company representative?

What would a just person do?

Is this story similar to Nirushan's?

A mos was another prophet who spoke out for justice. He was a simple peasant farmer and a shepherd in the desert wilderness near Tekoa in Judah. Amos cared for fig trees at times to make extra money.

God called Amos to speak out for justice because some of the conditions in the northern kingdom of Israel had become unacceptable to God.

Open your bible and read Amos 2.6-7. Discuss the message with your friends.
In your treasure book, write and decorate this beautiful message about justice:

Let justice flow like water,
and integrity like an unfailing stream.
                    (See Amos 5.24.)

We have a right

Read the United Nations Rights of the Child. With your friends, discuss the rights in light of justice.

The United Nations Rights of the Child

Children everywhere have the right to . . .

Affection, love, and understanding.

Adequate nutrition and medical care.

An education.

Full opportunity for play and recreation.

A name and nationality.

Special care if handicapped.

Priority for relief in time of disaster.

Learn to be a useful member of society and to develop individual abilities.

Be brought up in a spirit of peace and universal brotherhood.

Enjoy these rights regardless of race, colour, sex, religion, national or social origin.

Remember

"Whoever welcomes you welcomes me, and whoever welcomes me welcomes the one who sent me." (Matthew 10.40)

17 I was a stranger and you welcomed me

Welcome to Canada

After terrible hardship, Tan and Tran and their two children managed to get out of Vietnam. But they were boat people, with no money left after the boatman was paid. Worse, they no longer had ties with their relatives or their country. They were hungry, worried about the future, and fearful of pirates, who plunder poor people trying to escape to a new life. All the family saw for weeks was endless sea.

Still, they kept hoping that some generous country would take them in. And then, there was Canada: Halifax, Montreal, Saskatoon, Humboldt. The family was sponsored by the Franciscan Sisters of St. Elizabeth. Tran was to work as a cook in St. Elizabeth's Hospital.

"Right away, I like it," says Tran (not given to using the past tense), "but I don't like cold winters!" The children, however, have learned to enjoy the Saskatchewan snowdrifts.

"Tran and Tan have begun looking at Christianity," says Sister Clothilde. "They wanted to know more about Christians and their open hearts and open doors. Naturally," she explains, "the children want to do as their friends and go to church. But the parents are asking the deeper questions.

They are fascinated by the story of Jesus and his readiness to give up his life for others."

Tan and Tran are both exceptional cooks. Their new friends have been lucky because they have been treated to Vietnamese-style cooking. "It's almost worth a trip to Vietnam!" said one of their friends. Soon, such a trip won't be necessary, however.

"They're soon going to begin their own restaurant in Alberta," says Sister Dolores. "They're flying without our help but it's sad to see them go, because they've become part of our family."

Look up other stories of refugees who came to Canada. If possible, arrange an interview with one of them.

With your friends, check out Canada's current refugee policy and display your findings in your gathering space.

The man who wouldn't give

Jesus once told his followers this story about a rich man and Lazarus.

There was a rich man who used to dress in purple and fine linen and feast magnificently every day. And at his gate there lay a poor man called Lazarus, covered with sores, who longed to fill himself with the scraps that fell from the rich man's table. Dogs even came and licked his sores. The poor man died and was carried away by the angels to the bosom of Abraham. The rich man also died and was buried.

In his torment in Hades he looked up and saw Abraham a long way off with Lazarus in his bosom. So he cried out, "Father Abraham, pity me and send Lazarus to dip the tip of his finger in water and cool my tongue, for I am in agony in these flames." "My son," Abraham replied, "remember that during your life good things came your way, just as bad things came the way of Lazarus. Now he is being comforted here while you are in agony. But that is not all: between us and you a great gulf has been fixed, to stop anyone, if he wanted to, crossing from our side to yours, and to stop any crossing from your side to ours."

The rich man replied, "Father, I beg you then to send Lazarus to my father's house, since I have five brothers, to give them warning so that they do not come to this place of torment, too." "They have Moses and the prophets," said Abraham. "Let them listen to them." "Ah no, Father Abraham," said the rich man, "but if someone comes to them from the dead, they will repent."

Then Abraham said to him, "If they will not listen either to Moses or to the prophets, they will not be convinced even if someone should rise from the dead." (See Luke 16.19-31.)

Make a list of the contrasts in the story.
What do the rich man and the poor man have in common?
What differences are there between them?
What does this story have to do with hunger in our world?
What does this story have to do with welcoming the stranger?

111

A community challenge

Read this text from Matthew's gospel. What message is here for us? What does it say about God's call to justice?

"I was hungry and you gave me no food;
I was thirsty and you gave me nothing
to drink;
I was a stranger and you did not welcome me;
naked and you did not give me clothing,
sick and in prison and you did not
visit me. . . .
Truly I tell you,
just as you did not do it to one of the
least of these,
you did not do it to me."

(See Matthew 25.42-43; 45)

 Think about how your community responds to God's call. Examine the pictures and discuss the questions with your friends.

How does our community treat those who are sick?

How does our community care for the homeless?

How does our community take care of prisoners?

How does our community welcome strangers?

Prayers for justice

Get together with your friends and create prayers of petition for your basket of hope. Think about justice in our day-to-day relationships as you write your prayers. Use the basket to pray as a class. Add to your prayer basket throughout the year.

Remember

"I was hungry and you gave me food, I was thirsty and you gave me something to drink, I was a stranger and you welcomed me, I was naked and you gave me clothing, I was sick and you took care of me, I was in prison and you visited me." (Matthew 25.35-36)

18 Let justice flow like water

The earth is our home;
Her gifts give us life.

The air that we breathe,
the water we drink,
the land that we harvest.

We must care for these gifts;
They are fragile and free.
Surely a gift from our God!

An insight into ecology

Ecology refers to the study of how living creatures live together on this planet. Ecologists are concerned with taking care of the earth, respecting creation and the earth as home.

Read the message on page 114.

What does it say about our relationship with the earth?

How does it challenge us?

Now read the petition sent to the Canadian government by Our Lady of Fatima students in Renfrew, Ontario. What does it say about our relationship with the earth? What challenge does the petition present?

What kind of world do you want for the future?

COMMUNITY

The Pembroke Observer — Tues., June 21, 1988

Students' Petition Read in Commons

OTTAWA (Staff) — Students from Our Lady of Fatima School in Renfrew received some national exposure this week in the House of Commons.

The students asked MP Len Hopkins to read and present a petition that has been sent to Prime Minister Brian Mulroney.

In their petition the students state, "Through our studies we have become aware of the main causes of acid rain. Acid rain is promoted by an unnecessary use of electricity and fossil fuels. Both coal and oil are used in each of these cases. Coal and oil both contain sulfur and nitrogen which, when released into the air, combine with oxygen. In the clouds these pollutants undergo further changes, forming acid rain."

The students continue: "People might say we are just kids but we are not JUST kids. We are the adults of the future. We have rights, TOO! We have the right to crystal clear water to drink and to swim in. We have the right to catch fish that are not deformed. We have the right to have a clean world as God meant it to be."

"The students of Our Lady of Fatima School in Renfrew, Ontario, have asked me to impress upon the Prime Minister that he take their message seriously. May I respectfully request that he do so," said Mr. Hopkins.

(Reprinted with permission – *The Daily Observer*, Pembroke, Ontario, Canada.)

115

What is a habitat?

A habitat is a place where an animal or plant naturally lives or grows. It includes all that goes into making a home, with basic needs such as food, water, space and shelter.

A habitat refers to an environment or neighbourhood where a creature may live in comfort.

Take a look at the habitats on this page. They have been created by Grade 5 students as part of an ecological research project.

Pick a favourite animal and research its habitat. Determine its basic needs: food, water, space, shelter. Use a shoebox to create a habitat for your animal.

Mould your animal out of clay or Plasticine and place it in its habitat. You may create a puppet of your animal if you wish.

Design rules of care for your new friend.

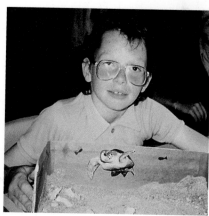

Our planet needs your help!

With your classmates, form investigative teams. Write reports about one of the following topics.

Wake-up call!

Fish stocks are declining. If we continue to overfish, certain species will disappear.

Research: What is happening to the fish stocks in the world's oceans? What is being done about it? What needs to be done?

Wake-up call!

Gases released in the atmosphere are affecting our climate.

Research: Find out how these gas emissions are affecting our climate. What is being done about it? What needs to be done?

Wake-up call!

The ozone layer, which protects us from the sun's harmful rays, is being destroyed.

Research: What are some problems being caused by the depletion of the ozone layer? What is being done about it? What needs to be done?

Wake-up call!

Garbage, garbage and more garbage! We are running out of storage space for our garbage.

Research: What are we going to do with all the wastes we are creating? What is being done about it? What needs to be done?

With your friends, visit a local beach or recreational area. List all the things you find that can be harmful to the environment. Collect at least five samples.

Arrange a display of these samples. Plan a forum to share all the information you have learned. Make suggestions for recycling.

Celebrate God's gift of creation

Wise and bountiful God,

you spread the table of creation
  before us.

Help us to appreciate the beauty
  of creation

and take responsibility for the
  care of the earth.

We ask this through our Lord Jesus
  Christ, your Son,

who lives and reigns with you in the
  unity of the Holy Spirit,

God forever and ever.

May the God who created the stars,

the sun and the moon,

earth, seas and sky,

the plants and animals,

men, women and children

bless us and be with us always.

[adapted from the *Liturgies of Lament*
by J. Frank Henderson]

new words

ecology: the branch of biology
that deals with the relationship
of living organisms to their
environment and to each other

habitat: the place where an animal
or plant naturally lives or grows

Remember
"Be fruitful, multiply, fill the earth
and subdue it." (Genesis 1.28)

Unit 7
The Church reconciles

19 God saw that it was good

Lent – a special time to prepare for Easter

During Lent, we prepare ourselves to celebrate that Jesus died and rose for us. The word Lent means "spring" or "change." It is a time when we take a look at ourselves and at our lives to see if we have lived up to our Baptism into God's Spirit. It is a time to examine our Christian roots, a time for renewal and conversion in our lives. During Lent, we look inside our lives and we change our hearts.

How will you and your friends journey through Lent?

What will you do to prepare for Easter?

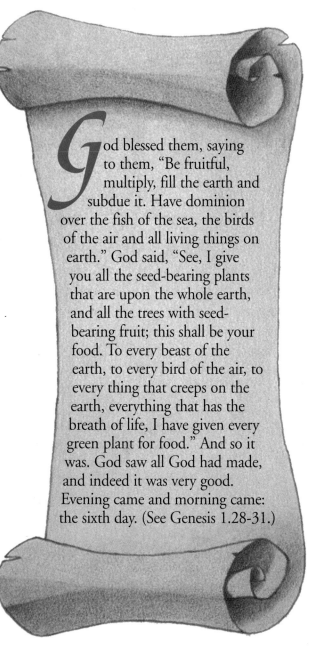

God blessed them, saying to them, "Be fruitful, multiply, fill the earth and subdue it. Have dominion over the fish of the sea, the birds of the air and all living things on earth." God said, "See, I give you all the seed-bearing plants that are upon the whole earth, and all the trees with seed-bearing fruit; this shall be your food. To every beast of the earth, to every bird of the air, to every thing that creeps on the earth, everything that has the breath of life, I have given every green plant for food." And so it was. God saw all God had made, and indeed it was very good. Evening came and morning came: the sixth day. (See Genesis 1.28-31.)

Ecology recommendations

1. People who litter should be held responsible for their actions.

2. We should protect our animal life and make sure that those who illegally kill our animal life will be prosecuted.

3. Atomic warfare must be banned.

4. Toxic wastes must be safely stored.

5. Animals should be treated as humans wish to be treated.

6. Once a week try to clean up a part of our neighbourhood.

7. Humans should respect the life of other humans.

8. Recycling must expand in order to preserve our natural resources.

9. Students must be made aware of our ecological problems so they can begin to solve these problems.

10. Industry and government must become more responsible for the disposal of waste.

From the Ojibway people
The Creation

The water began to rise and to circle in muddy swirls. The sky was covered with clouds that dropped torrential rains. The entire neighbourhood was flooded, then half of the earth, and in the end the whole wide world was covered with water.

On the following day Menaboju saw the stiff corpse of a small muskrat floating toward him in the waves. He caught him, took him in his hands, and put life back into him, blowing his warm breath on him. Then he said to him, "Little brother Rat, neither of us can live without the earth. Dive down in the water and bring me some soil if you can."

The obliging little animal dived down immediately and came back to the surface after a long time. Menaboju caught the little body and examined its paws. In one of the front paws he discovered a few grains of sand. He took them out of the paw, put them on his palm, and dried them in the sun. Then he blew them away across the water; wherever they fell, they floated on the surface. They grew and expanded. First of all, the little islands were formed, then they expanded quickly and grew together to form larger ones.

Diligently and actively, Menaboju marched back and forth, arranging everything and setting up nature in its former beauty. Many stiff animal corpses were washed up onto the beach. Menaboju picked up all of them and blew life into them. Then he said to them, "Leave for your places at once." And so each animal went to its place.

The earth that had been created by Menaboju in this manner was the first land in this world inhabited by Indians.

(Kohl, J.G. *Kitchi-gami: Life among the Lake Superior Ojibwayi.*
London, England: Chapman and Hale, 1860.)

How does Menaboju take great care in creating the earth?

**Take a piece of soil in your hands. Mould and shape it into a form.
Let it be your piece of creation.**

A class pictograph

This pictograph is located north of Lake Superior at the Agawa site. It is part of a story involving a medicine man called Myeengun (Wolf) who undertook a hazardous voyage.

Do you know what *petroglyphs* are? A petroglyph is a picture that is carved in rock. The word comes from two Greek words: *petros*, which means "a stone," and *glypho*, which means "I carve." Prehistoric people used petroglyphs to tell their stories and to express symbols of their lives. About 34 miles northeast of Peterborough, Ontario, in the middle of the Kawartha Lake district, is the largest collection of native petroglyphs in North America! Research these petroglyphs. Who do they belong to? When were they carved?

Pictographs are different from petroglyphs. They are pictures that are painted on rock. These, too, were used by prehistoric people to tell stories about their lives.

Think about your class rock for a moment. Imagine a team of researchers finding it millions of years from now. What would they think? How would they interpret it? What would they do with it?

Take a rock of your choice and paint a creation scene on it. Present it to one of your friends or a family member as an Easter gift.

Remember

In the beginning God created the heavens and the earth . . . and God saw that it was good. (See Genesis 1.1, 10.)

20 God's faithfulness is from age to age

The Fall

The man and the woman were very happy in the garden. They were intimate friends of God. It is said that God walked with them in the garden in the cool of the evening.

Then one day the serpent tempted the woman, saying, "Did God really tell you not to eat the fruit of any of the trees in the garden?"

The woman replied, "No. We may eat the fruit of the trees in the garden. There is one, however, that we must not eat. God said that if we eat this fruit, we will die."

"You won't die if you eat the fruit of this tree," the serpent responded. "God knows that if you eat of this tree your eyes will be opened and you will be like gods, knowing good and evil."

The woman looked at the tree. It was full of fruit and beautiful. She reached toward the tree, plucked the fruit and ate it. She turned toward the man who was beside her and gave him some fruit. He ate it, too.

(See Genesis 3.1-8.)

What does God do in the face of evil? Finish the story.

Psalms of trust

O God, you are my rock
strong, worthy, like a good friend,
you are right beside me when troubles occur
I can trust you for help and love.
Owen

God, you are like an eagle
strong, free, swift and slow to anger.
God, you are like a rock,
no evil can get through you.

God, you are like a lion
always showing your power and trust.
God, you are like a cheetah,
swift and sure-footed.
Melissa

O God, I want you to know that I love you
and believe in you with all my heart,
I trust you with my secrets and promises
I believe in you and love you.
Jeanette

Like water that flows down the river
my trust flows strong and free,
like the river
my trust will not stop flowing.
Michael

O Lord, my God and friend,
to me, you're like the wind,
blowing gently through the sand,
blowing gently on my hand.

And on my face and through
   my hair,
you and I, God, are like a pair
of soft-feathered birds flying
   through the air
O Lord, my God and friend.
Cathy

God, you are like a rock
no evil can go through you,
you are very strong
like a wall of gold.
Frank

**Use the blackline master
that your teacher gives
you and write your own
psalm of trust.**

When we are tempted

Read Matthew 4.1-11. What did Jesus do when he was tempted? What did he say? Write his words in your treasure book.

You are at the mall with your mom. She picks out a pair of gym shoes for you. They are the cheaper brand. Your heart is set on the popular brand. Most of your friends have them. But they are much more expensive. What do you do?

You are sitting in class doing a math test. You know you have not studied enough for the test. You want to do well. Your friend's paper is just across the way, on the edge of her desk. You know she studied hard. What do you do?

What do you do?

Kim Lak comes from Cambodia. She is alone most of the time. You want to get to know her but you know your friends have not welcomed her. What do you do?

I set my bow in the clouds

The people of the earth grew in sin and wickedness. The earth became more and more corrupt. God looked at the earth and came to regret having made the earth and especially its people. God's heart was full of sorrow. God said, "The earth is full of violence. I will rid the earth's face of people."

But on the earth there lived a good and just man named Noah. He walked with God. God commissioned him one day to build an ark and take his family and a pair of all living creatures aboard. Noah did what God asked. It began to rain. It rained for forty days and nights. The floods were so severe that all living creatures of the earth perished. Only Noah, his family and the creatures of the ark survived.

When the floods ended, God said to Noah, "Come out of the ark, you yourself, your wife, your sons and your son's wives with you…. Let all the animals swim on the earth; let them be fruitful and multiply on the earth." And Noah did what God commanded. Noah then built an altar for God and offered a sacrifice to God. God smelled the offering and said, "Never again will I curse the earth because of what people do."

And God made a covenant with Noah and his family and with all their descendants. "Never again will I destroy all living things by the waters of the flood…. Here is the sign of the covenant between myself and you and every living creature with you for all generations: I set my bow in the clouds and it shall be a sign of the covenant between me and the earth."

With your friends, discuss how this story shows that God's love is everlasting.

Create a litany of praise and thanks to God using the refrain "God's love is everlasting."

Remember

"I set my bow in the clouds and it shall be a sign of the covenant between me and the earth." (See Genesis 9.14.)

21 The Spirit of Jesus reconciles the world

Close call

"Johnny, do you remember the time you almost drowned?" his mom asked. And so Johnny began to tell his story.

"We had just settled in for another camping season at the river. So there were lots of things to be done.

"The river was really high that year and Dad said we couldn't go swimming yet. But we could paddle around in our homemade kayaks near the shore. One afternoon Joe and I thought we would surprise Dad by stringing our safety rope across the river at the usual place, just below our swimming hole but just above the rapids. If any swimmer got in trouble, there was a rope to grab. This way no one would be swept into the rapids.

"So Joe and I tied one end of the rope on a tree. I volunteered to cross the river. I tied the other end to my ankle, because I couldn't paddle and hold the rope at the same time. Well, there I was, almost to the other side in my little kayak! But the river was much wider that year. Suddenly, I realized I had run out of rope!

"It all happened in a flash! My kayak overturned and I found myself being swept down into the rapids. I would be upside down one minute and then up for air the next. I felt scared. I knew I was in trouble. I remember thinking about others who had drowned in the river. I was going to be next!

"Then suddenly I wasn't moving anymore! The water was rushing around me but I was up against something solid. My head bobbed just above water. I was lodged against a big, firm rock. Somehow, I felt sheltered and protected. Then I looked toward the shore and saw Dad at the other end of the rope. He looked scared. He started to wade into the water.

"'Dad, don't come!' I yelled. 'Just get me in.' I felt sure Dad would save me."

At this point, Johnny's dad, Ken, took up the story:

"I guess I wasn't thinking very clearly. I just wanted to get to him and save him. But now I know if I had gone any further, I too would have been swept away by the current and the two of us would have drowned. As Johnny struggled to get the rope untied from his ankle, I worked out a plan. We had to pull him from rock to rock and bring him up on shore."

Johnny continued. "I felt I was being pulled in like a fish!" The room was quiet. Then, turning to his dad, Johnny said, "You saved me, Dad!"

Ken, looking around at his family and friends, responded very simply, "Thanks to the rock, we're all here!"

How must Johnny have felt, discovering he had no more rope? clinging to the rock? being reunited with his family?
Do you have a story like Johnny's to share?
Draw a picture of Johnny on shore, safe with his family.

I am the living water

Jesus left Judaea and headed back to Galilee. On the way he came to the Samaritan town called Sychar, near the land that Jacob gave his son Joseph. Jacob's well is there and Jesus, tired by the journey, sat straight down by the well. It was about the sixth hour. When a Samaritan woman came to draw water, Jesus said to her, "Give me a drink." His disciples had gone into the town to buy food. The Samaritan woman said to him, "What? You are a Jew and you ask me, a Samaritan, for a drink?" (For Jews had no dealings with Samaritans.) Jesus replied,

"If you knew the gift of God and who it is that is saying to you:
'Give me a drink,'
you would have been the one to ask,
and he would have given you living water."

"You have no bucket, sir," she answered, "and the well is deep. Where do you get this living water?"

(See John 4.3-11.)

Finish the story in your treasure book. To help you, read John 4.16-42.
What does Jesus do? How do Jesus' words and actions affect the woman?
How do his words affect the community? How is the story about reconciliation?

A visual journal of our lives

Take a look at the masks on this page. Grade 5 students have created these to help them look inward and reflect on their lives. Follow the blackline master your teacher gives you and choose a mask for your Lenten reflection.

Throughout Lent, use the mask to record words, actions, changes, sad and happy things that happen to you. In this way, your mask will become a visual journal of your life. Complete your mask during the Easter break. Bring it with you when you return to school after Easter. You and your friends will be invited to share the symbols and stories of your masks during an Easter party.

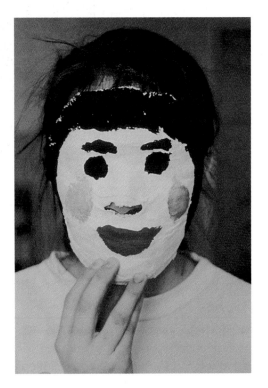

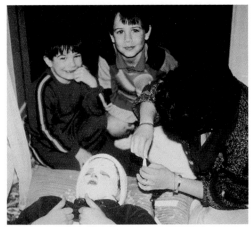

Give me another chance

Have you ever had a time in your life when you were given another chance? Did you ever argue with a friend, then make up again? How did it feel to be in conflict? How did it feel to reconcile?

In Baptism, we enter into God's reconciliation. In the sacrament of Eucharist, we celebrate God's reconciliation. There is, however, another way that God reconciles us again and again: through the sacrament of Reconciliation. Check out these questions to see what you remember about this sacrament:

Where do we celebrate the sacrament of Reconciliation?
What happens?
What is your role?
What is the priest's role?
What is the community's role?
What does God do?

Rite of reconciliation

There are three forms of the rite of reconciliation. Do you know what they are? Look at the steps outlined here:

- Welcoming the penitent
- Reading the word of God
- Confessing sins
- Praying for God's pardon and absolution
- Praising God
- Dismissing the penitent

Which form of the rite do these steps belong to?

In your treasure book, briefly describe the importance of each step. Share your description with your friends.

How do we give praise and thanks to God in the sacrament of Reconciliation?

A circle prayer

Creator God,
Your circle of love is broken
whenever there is no love,
no justice,
no peace.

Forgive us
for the many times
we have broken
the circle of love
by our words,
our deeds,
our attitudes.

Forgive us
for the many times
we have failed
to stand together
as friends.

Send your Holy Spirit
upon us at Easter
so that our anger will turn
into peace,
our sadness into joy,

our fears into comfort,
so that our circle
will become one —
single and unbroken,
wide open and welcoming.

Loving God, bless us,
embrace us and send
us forth renewed so that we
become
instruments of your peace.
In the power of
your Spirit, may we be
leaders of your
generosity and joy.

May we live each day in
the name of God
and include all in our
circle of love. This
we ask through Jesus Christ
our Lord, in
the Holy Spirit.

Amen.

Remember

"Very truly, I tell you, no one can enter the kingdom of God without being born of water and Spirit." (John 3.5)

Unit 8
The Church loves

22 Love as I have loved you

Finish the stories

Stranded

Nicole and her infant daughter, Patrice, are driving home late at night. Suddenly, about 10 km from their home, the car begins to sputter and lose speed. Nicole tries to keep the motor running but it doesn't help. The dashboard lights up with the red glow of a warning signal and the engine sputters to a stop.

Nicole guides the vehicle off to the side of the road. What is she going to do now? She and Patrice had dressed for a warm spring day when they left home. Now, with the car stopped, she can feel the cold, chilly air creeping in through the windows. Cold and worried, Nicole gets out of the car to try to get one of the oncoming vehicles to stop.

Three vehicles come by. They are driven by
a) a nurse rushing to the hospital to begin the late shift;
b) a lawyer returning from a service club meeting;
c) a biker out for a spin, checking the exhaust system on a new bike . . .

The runaway

Megan and Sarah lived with their father in a small apartment over his shop. He depended on the girls to help him with different jobs, such as answering the phone. Because the business was small and new, there was little money for anything more than necessities.

The father wanted his girls to have everything, but he couldn't afford much. Because he knew the girls enjoyed music, he bought them a CD player with some of their favourite CDs. He really needed a copier for his office, but he decided to treat the girls instead.

One evening, Sarah stayed to watch a football game after school. Because she was not home to answer the phone, her father lost a very important business contract. Her dad punished her by forbidding her to use the CD player for a full month.

The next morning Sarah didn't go to school. After Megan left and her father went to work, Sarah packed up the CD player and CDs, and with all the money she could find called a taxi to take her to the airport. A one-way ticket to the city was all she needed.

One day a few weeks later, the phone rang in the little shop. It was a collect call. "I want to come home, Dad," Sarah sobbed. "I have no money and I want to come home."

Finish the stories as you think they might unfold.

Settling accounts

The school was planning a camping trip. There was one rule, however. The students were to earn the money themselves and not ask their parents or friends to contribute.

Everyone started looking for a way to earn money. Darren and Todd went to Mr. LeBlanc and asked if they could do some work for him. He told them he would pay them each $10.00 to clean out his barn on Saturday morning.

Saturday morning, Mr. LeBlanc showed the boys all of the newspapers, tins and jars that he had stored in his barn. A new recycling depot had opened, and he wanted the boys to box everything for recycling.

The boys tackled the mountain of work. By eleven o'clock, however, they had only cleared a small space. But Mr. LeBlanc was very pleased and asked if they knew anyone who could help them finish by the end of the day. Darren called Jonathan and his sister, Melanie, who came over right away. Todd called his sister Jessica and her friend Trisha. They finished their chores at home and arrived on the scene at one o'clock. Everyone worked very hard into the afternoon.

About four o'clock, the very last bottle was picked up and the floor was swept clean. Mr. LeBlanc was happy and surprised. He didn't think they could finish all that work in one day! "Now, to reward you for your efforts," he said.

Finish this story by telling how much you think Mr. LeBlanc paid each of the workers.

God's love is like . . .

Luke 10.25-37

Luke 15.11-32

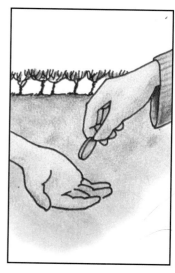

Matthew 20.1-16

Examine what is happening in the scenes and draw your own conclusions. Give each scene a title.

What do these scenes tell you about the love of God? Check out the parables in your Bible.

Create a series of comics entitled "God's love is like . . . ."

Choose examples from the parables.

Choose examples from the life and actions of Jesus.

Choose favourite personal examples.

Consider it your parable series.

Luke 13.10-17   Matthew 15.32-39   Luke 7.1-10

Examine what is happening in the scenes and draw your own conclusions. Give each scene a title.

What do these scenes tell you about the love of God? Check out the miracle stories in your Bible.

With your friends, discuss how God is with people in the event (seen through Jesus' example).

Prepare a shadow drama of the events.

Remember

God's love for us is superabundant. Through parables, Jesus tells us about God's love. Jesus, too, is a parable of God's love.

23 I have given you an example

One of the earth's most valuable resources is oil. Explorers drill deep into the earth and under the ocean in search of this precious resource.

Why do people go to such efforts to find oil? Why is it so valuable? What are its many uses?

Go on an "oil dig" in your school, at home, throughout your community. Make a list of the various ways we use oil.

Arrange a visit with your parish priest to see the special oils used in the church.

How do Christians use oil?
When are the oils blessed?
Who blesses the oils?
What happens to the oils after they are blessed?

Draw a picture in your treasure book showing how we use oil in our faith tradition.

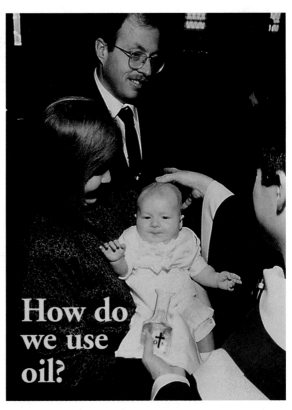

How do we use oil?

Anointed with the Holy Spirit

 Look at the picture.
How is oil used? Why?

Use the references below to find the uses of oil in Scripture. Based on the special uses of oil in your scripture passages, identify the heading under which your passages should go:

- **anointing of kings**
- **priests**
- **the sick**
- **objects**
- **anointing with the Holy Spirit**

Identify what is common in all the texts.

How is oil used?

Group I
- I Samuel 10.1
- I Samuel 16.11-13
- Acts 10.38

Group II
- Mark 6.13
- James 5.14
- Acts 10.38

Group III
- Leviticus 8.12
- Exodus 30.30
- Acts 10.38

Group IV
- Genesis 28.18
- Exodus 30.25-29
- Acts 10.38

Group V
- Hebrews 1.9
- 2 Corinthians 1.21-22
- Acts 10.38

Anointed in God's Spirit

Read Jesus' mission statement on the scroll.

Do you remember when and where Jesus proclaimed this statement?

Which prophet is Jesus quoting?

The spirit of the Lord has been given to me,
for he has anointed me.
He has sent me to bring the good news to
the poor,
to proclaim liberty to captives
and to the blind new sight,
to set the downtrodden free,
to proclaim the Lord's year of favour.

(See Luke 4.16-21.)

What does an anointed person do?
What does Jesus do?
How does Jesus do it?
What do we do as God's anointed ones?

Bishop Eugene writes to us about Orders

Dear Students:

This theme is going to talk about how Jesus invites and helps all of us, his disciples, to build up his Body in the world. You know that you are a member of the Body of Jesus Christ in the world, through your Baptism.

Jesus needs each member of his Body to speak and act in the world. He needs you and me to show his face to the world and to tell others of his Father's faithful love for everyone. Especially, Jesus needs you and me to help the world remember that he died and was raised from the dead, so that we and all people could have eternal life.

Now, Jesus the Lord calls and ordains some of his disciples to be priests and bishops in his Body, the Church. They act "in his Person" by preaching the Good News of his death and resurrection, by celebrating the holy Eucharist and by leading his people.

We all have important work to do each day so that Jesus Christ's Body will be a vital and powerful presence in the world.

I am praying that you will remember each day your dignity and your task to walk with Jesus our Lord and, by the power of his Spirit, to build up his Body in the world.

Peace and care in Jesus, our risen Lord,

+Eugene J. Cooney

Eugene J. Cooney
Bishop of Nelson

Remember

Anointed with God's Spirit, we follow the way of Jesus.

24 We ponder the mystery of God's love

It is finished

A passion play in three scenes

By Brendan J. McCarthy

Scene One

The scene is set in a large room. A long table and benches occupy centre stage. A window is in the rear wall. On-stage, as the curtain opens, are two disciples, James and Andrew. They are seated on benches beside the table.

James: What a mess we made of everything! I never ran harder than I did last night getting out of that garden.

Andrew: When Peter cut off that fellow's ear, I thought we were in for it.

James: If the Master hadn't healed it, I'm sure we all would have died. I never saw a mob so angry.

Andrew: Yes, Peter always was quick to act. I knew he'd get us in trouble someday. I wonder where he went after we fled?

James: I was too busy running to notice. I don't even know where young John went. My father always told me to keep an eye on John. I hope he's safe.

Andrew: The Master's so fond of him. I feel that John might be brave enough to have followed him.

James: John may have gone along because he knows many of the people in the High Priest's household. We've sold them fish many times.

(There is a sound of hurried footsteps [stage right], the sound of a door opening, and a muffled figure rushes in. James and Andrew jump up in alarm and rush towards the left of the stage.)

Peter: Don't run, it's only me.

(Andrew and James stop and face the newcomer, who uncovers his face.)

Andrew: Where have you been? We were worried about you. We thought that the guards had caught you and were making you pay for cutting off Malchus' ear.

Peter: No, I ran too fast for that. But I did go to the High Priest's house with John.

James: Oh! Peter, where is he now? I've been so worried about him.

142

Peter: I don't know where he is now, but he brought me into the courtyard because he knew the doorman. He left me then to talk to some fellows he knew. I wish he'd stayed because I made a fool of myself afterwards.

Andrew: You're constantly doing that! What happened this time?

Peter: I was standing in the courtyard, trying to look as though I belonged there, when a servant girl said, "You were also with him." I was scared so I told her she was mistaken. She went away, but came back and told me she had seen me with Jesus once. I was really scared so I said she was wrong.

James: Why didn't you leave?

Peter: There were so many people around! I tried to find a dark corner but she found me again and told me that she knew from my Galilean accent that I was one of his men. Several guards were now looking suspiciously in my direction, so I swore an oath that I didn't know the fellow.

Andrew: But Peter, how could you do such a thing after Jesus made you his right-hand man?

Peter: Easy for you to say! But remember, you ran from the garden, too. I'm no hero, but now I have to live down the fact I betrayed his trust in me.

James: Where was Jesus while this was going on?

Peter: I didn't realize he heard me, but there he was and he looked at me . . .

that's when I fled. I never again want to see the look on his face.

(From outside in the distance shouts are heard.)

James: What's that?

(Andrew goes to the window and opens it. The shouting is clearer now: "Crucify him! Crucify him!")

Andrew:

(*horrified*) Oh God! It can't be true! They're calling for him to be crucified. Do you hear the shouting from Pilate's courtyard?

(Peter slumps into a chair and buries his face.)

James: How can the leaders of the people justify what they are doing? *(pause)* The next thing they will be wanting is to kill us as well. Close the window, Andrew. They'd better not find us here.

Scene Two

This scene is set in the courtyard of Pilate. There is a platform, stage left, with a curtain behind it. There is a crowd on the stage shouting.

The crowd: Bring him out! Let us see him! We don't want him for our king!

(Curtain behind the platform opens and Pilate emerges, followed by Jesus, who is being guarded by a Roman soldier.)

Pilate: Behold your king!

Someone in the crowd: He's not our king! Caesar is our king!

Pilate: But he said he is the king of the Jews.

Someone in the crowd: Away with the fellow! Crucify him! We have no king but Caesar!

Pilate: So you want me to crucify your king!

Crowd: Crucify him! He's a troublemaker.

Pilate: But I find no case against this man.

Someone in the crowd: If you let him go, you're not Caesar's friend.

Pilate: You brought this man before me as a troublemaker. Now I have gone into the matter myself and found him innocent of all the charges. The man has done nothing that deserves death! I'll have him flogged and let him go! *(exits, with guard and Jesus)*

(The crowd mills around, with occasional outbursts of anger. Pilate returns in a few moments with Jesus and his guard. The crowd hushes and turns once more to the platform.)

Pilate: Look, I had him scourged to teach him a lesson.

Crowd: Crucify him! Crucify him! Crucify him!

Pilate: I will not crucify him.

Someone in the crowd: We have a law and according to that law, he deserves to die.

(Pilate turns and speaks to the guard, who leaves and returns with a small basin of water and a towel. During the guard's absence, the crowd still chants various remarks about crucifying Jesus. There is a hush when the guard returns with water and towel. Pilate washes his hands.)

Pilate: I wash my hands of the blood of this just man. I will not be responsible for his death.

Crowd: Crucify him! Away with him!

(Pilate leaves the platform followed by Jesus and the guard.)

Scene Three

This scene is set on the hill of Calvary. It is after the crucifixion. The body of Jesus [centre] has just been taken down from the cross by Nicodemus and Joseph of Arimathea. The centurion and two soldiers are on one side of the stage. Behind Joseph and Nicodemus are John and Mary, Jesus' mother.

Joseph: *(crouched beside the body, which is completely wrapped in a white sheet)* Mary, we must go now to the tomb. The Sabbath approaches.

Mary: *(leaving John, and coming centre stage to where the body lies)* Allow me to receive his body once again and lay it to rest among the dead.

John: *(approaching Mary)* Yes, come and let us bury him. On this night we remember how God once passed over our people and saved us in the land of Egypt. May God also save this poor friend of ours.

Joseph: I have a tomb nearby. Let's put him there.

Mary: Yes, go ahead. There's little time left.

(Mary exits, leaning on John's arm, followed by Nicodemus and Joseph carrying the shrouded body.)

Nicodemus: May he not dwell in darkness but be welcomed into God's own light!

1st soldier: I hope that's the end of it. These people always think they are messengers of their God.

Centurion: I don't know. This was no ordinary man we crucified today. All of a sudden it was dark as night. I think it had something to do with his death.

2nd soldier: Sir, do you think all the things they say about this man were true?

Centurion: What things?

2nd soldier: Well, one man told me he saw this fellow feed large crowds of people.

1st soldier: Yes, and I was told he actually cured the sick and cared for them.

Centurion: Come to think of it, Centurion Publius of the Third Legion told me he heard only last week that this Jesus raised a man to life over in Bethany.

2nd soldier: *(laughing)* Sir, don't you think that's going a bit too far? Who ever heard of anyone being raised from the dead?

Centurion: Publius is not a person given to gossip, and he swore that his source was trustworthy.

1st soldier: I don't know anything about raising the dead, but I do know that this man was something special. I heard him say something about forgiving people…

2nd soldier: That would be a first! We certainly wouldn't expect that.

Centurion: I have seen many men die by crucifixion, but this one has me puzzled. Anyway, all this talk will not get your work done. Get to it! *(Soldiers go about their work. The centurion moves to one side, and muses.)* Could it be true? Could this man be what his followers claimed him to be: the Messiah, the Son of God? If this is so, then it is not the end of the story.

Think about the centurion's closing words in the drama. Is the crucifixion the end of the story? Or is it just the beginning?

God's love for us was revealed when God sent into the world God's only Son so that we could have life through him; that is the love I mean: not our love for God, but God's love for us when God sent Jesus to be the sacrifice that takes our sins away. (See I John 4.9-10.)

Venerating the cross.

 How is the cross a symbol of sacrifice? How is it a symbol of God's love? How is it a symbol of life through death?

Remember

Behold the wood of the cross.

Unit 9
The Church rejoices

25 Were not our hearts burning within us?

We are an Easter people
and alleluia is our song!
We are an Easter people
and alleluia, alleluia,
alleluia is our song!

A masquerade of stories

The squiggled line shows that I took sick suddenly and had to be rushed to hospital. The balloon on my mask represents my birthday which was on Holy Thursday. The hand shows that I tried to help people more. The shamrock shows that I am Irish. The neck collar tells you that I took care of my cat. The heart tells you that I tried to be more friendly to others.

Erin

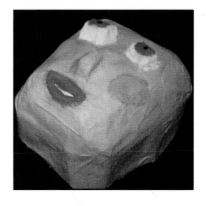

My symbols include smiling with love, being a friend, Christianity and spring showers.

Kim

Two weeks ago my friend Dana stayed at my house. Late in the evening she started to cry, because my sister was sort of mad at her. I comforted Dana until she was all right again.

Leia

I went tobogganing with my sister. We had only one toboggan. My sister wanted to try the hill first. So did I. I let her go first. It made her happy.

Daniel

Two of my friends were having a big argument. It just seemed to go on forever. It grew bigger and bigger. I decided to step in and help them clear it up. It worked. Now all three of us go together to the gym again.

Patrick

Share the story of your mask with your friends.

Easter symbols

Easter fire

Even before the time of Christ, people used to say that the sun dies each night and rises again in the morning. Therefore, the early Christians used the sun's rising as a symbol of Christ's resurrection. The custom of blessing a new fire at Easter began hundreds of years ago. At the Easter Vigil we light the new fire, the Paschal candle. From this flame the candles of all who participate in the ceremony are lit, lighting the darkened church with the light of Christ.

Easter water

Many centuries ago people thought that water had special power. Each spring they saw ice turn to flowing, life-giving water. They bathed in this new water, believing it would make them stronger and more powerful. Water refreshes and renews us and thus is a sign of our new life in Christ received at Baptism. Baptisms often take place at the Easter Vigil, and all present are reminded of new life in Christ by renewing baptismal promises.

Easter clothing

The custom of wearing our best outfits at Easter began in the early centuries of Christianity. Those baptized at the Easter Vigil wore white robes during Easter week to symbolize their new life in Christ. Other Christians tried to wear new clothes to show that they, too, had risen to new life – not only through Baptism but also by their prayers, fasting and almsgiving during Lent.

Easter bread

Bread is a basic food, "the staff of life." In some countries, a beautifully decorated round loaf of bread called *pascha* is an important Easter symbol. Along with other Easter foods, this pascha is blessed at Easter time. For families who gather for breakfast after the Easter liturgy, this bread is a sign of their being united in the life of the risen Lord. As they share the bread, they recall these words of Jesus:

> *"I am the bread of life . . .*
> *whoever comes to me will never be hungry."*
> (See John 6.35.)

Easter egg

The egg looks like a stone until suddenly it cracks and out of the stone comes the warm, soft body of a living creature. For this reason, eggs are symbols of new life. For hundreds of years, Christians have used them as a symbol of the resurrection of Christ. Just as the shell is broken for new life to come out, the rock at the tomb was rolled away at Jesus' resurrection.

The pisanka

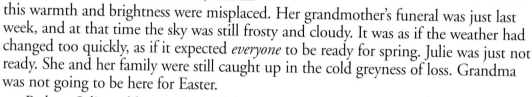

To everybody else, spring was in the air. The breeze was warm, the trees were showing purple-red buds waiting to burst open, the birds were noisily going about their nest-building. Spring was everywhere, except at Julie's house.

For Julie, especially, it seemed that the world was somehow out of order, that all this warmth and brightness were misplaced. Her grandmother's funeral was just last week, and at that time the sky was still frosty and cloudy. It was as if the weather had changed too quickly, as if it expected *everyone* to be ready for spring. Julie was just not ready. She and her family were still caught up in the cold greyness of loss. Grandma was not going to be here for Easter.

Perhaps Julie and her mother didn't really feel like preparing the *pisankas*, the special Easter eggs, that afternoon. But Easter was only a few days away, and a tradition is a tradition. "After all," her mother reasoned as they prepared the colours for the eggs, "Easter only comes once a year. We can't just forget about it. What would Grandma say?"

What would Grandma say? Julie remembered that when it came to preparing the pisankas, Grandma would say very little for a long time. She would concentrate very hard on every little detail of the egg decorating. She would hold the egg gently but firmly, so that it wouldn't slip. The egg Julie took now seemed so light, and she thought of the robins who were flapping around the lower branches of the tree outside. They, too, would have eggs soon.

Julie traced a fine line completely around her egg and then retraced it until she didn't know where she had started. "Eternity," Grandma had once said. "You can go around and around and never stop. That's a symbol in the decorating." In arithmetic, Julie's class had talked about eternity, always adding on one more number. The idea had made her head ache. Going on and on and on seemed like such a frustration. Today, as she looked at the line around the egg she held, eternity seemed more comfortable. She traced another line around the egg, just because it felt good to do so.

After a while, Julie realized how hard she had been concentrating, how long she had been wrapped in thought. "Mom's been quiet, too," she thought, and left her chair to watch over her mother's shoulder. Delicately, her mother traced a cross on the egg she was working with. Julie watched silently, remembering how Grandma had said that every symbol on the pisanka held a deep meaning. In her mother's hands, a simple egg was transformed into something special, something that spoke of Christ's dying and rising. Something, too, that spoke of Grandma.

"You like it?" her mother said at last. "It's pretty good, I think. So, this one will be for you. Pisankas are to be given as gifts of love. This will be my gift to you. What should be put on it next?" Her mother hesitated for only a split second. "What would Grandma do with it next, do you suppose?"

Julie realized that she was smiling. And her mom was smiling, too, a soft relaxed smile. They hadn't been relaxing or smiling much lately!

Julie walked over to the window, to let in the sounds of springtime.

What do you think the last line of the story shows about the change in Julie?
Draw a picture of Julie at this moment.

Celebrate the Easter season

Long ago in eastern Europe, decorating eggs with Easter symbols became an art. It also became a prayer, because as people carefully decorated the eggs, they reflected on the Easter mystery in the stories of Jesus' Passion, death and resurrection. At Easter the eggs were brought to church, blessed and given to relatives and special friends. When Christians exchange these as gifts, they give one another a gift of prayer, as well as a sign of God's gift of new life in Christ.

Today, carefully designed and decorated hollow or blown-out eggs can be works of art suitable for gifts at any time of the year. Since the Easter season lasts a full 50 days, prepare your own blown-out egg and decorate it. Give it to a friend or member of your family to remind them that we are still in the Easter season.

Follow the directions on the blackline master your teacher will give you. If you wish, use the pisanka design to decorate your egg.

Remember
The Lord has risen indeed, alleluia!

26 Christians are Easter people

Show and tell

Think about what it is to be you! Imagine being asked to identify who you are. What story would you tell? What symbol or action would you choose to express your identity?

Read these identity stories. What are the symbols?

My name is Koran. My favourite talent is Karate. I am a red two.

Hi. My name is Patricia. I like to play soccer. I'm pretty good at keeping the ball out of the net.

My name is Jade. I love to sing. It's what I do the best.

Join with your friends in playing an identity game. Prepare your story and symbol.

Think for a moment about your class. How would you identify it if someone asked? What story and symbol would you choose?

We are Easter people

 Think for a moment about how we become Easter people. How do Easter people identify themselves? What story do they tell? What action or symbol do they share?

Read the words on the easel. Do you know what Christians call this event? It is the **paschal mystery**. When Christians celebrate their Easter identity, that is the story they tell. It is the story of what God has done for us in Jesus.

With your friends, prepare an easel similar to the one on this page. Write the words "the life, death, resurrection and coming in glory of the Lord Jesus" on the easel. Decorate your easel.

The life, death, resurrection and coming in glory of the Lord Jesus.

A sacrament centre

The sacraments are the Church's celebration of the paschal mystery in which God sets us free and recreates us. The paschal mystery holds the sacraments together.

Make your own sacrament centre.

Draw a picture for each sacrament. Describe what the Church does when it comes together to celebrate the sacraments. Show how the pattern of each sacrament is the same. We hear the word of God and perform the ritual action in faith.

Make a mobile of the essential actions that are part of each sacrament. Group together the initiation sacraments – Baptism, Confirmation and Eucharist. Show that the other sacraments flow from these.

Place your easel in a central place in the sacrament centre.

An Easter people mosaic

 Develop an Easter people mosaic for your sacrament centre. Begin by cutting a large circle from construction paper. Print these words at the centre of the circle: "the life, death, resurrection and coming in glory of the Lord Jesus."

Next, collect photos of Easter people in action in your community: home, parish, school, and diocese. Look especially for photos of Baptism, Confirmation and Eucharist.

Place photos of people celebrating the initiation sacraments around the centre of the circle. Next, add the rest of the photos of Easter people in action. This will create a ring-like effect.

As you learn more about the sacraments and meet other Easter people, represent them on your mosaic. Add to it throughout the rest of the year.

new words

paschal mystery: refers to the life, death, resurrection and coming in glory of the Lord Jesus

Remember

In the sacraments, the paschal mystery is made present in the power of the Holy Spirit.

27 We meet Easter people

A lamp in the snow

He was only a boy, and he had seen very little beyond the farm where he lived with his family. But Omer Robidoux often thought about the people of the North. Often, as he was doing his work on the farm, he would think about them, about what wise people the Inuit were. These people of the open country, of the barren land – they knew how to build a warm, safe house, how to build a kayak for the seal hunt, where to find the partridge once it had lost its summer feathers and turned pure white, like snow. The more he thought about it, the more Omer realized how self-sufficient these people really were. He wondered if he could do anything for them.

A secret voice kept calling. If only he could become a priest, Omer could teach the people of the North about Jesus, God's Son, who walked among the people and loved them and cured those who were sick. Yes, Omer could tell the people that Jesus suffered and died and that he rose from the dead. He could tell them that Jesus is alive, that he loves us and cares for us and wants us to live forever with him in heaven.

When Omer Robidoux grew to be a young man, he decided to become a missionary priest and work with the people of the North. He would have to be a man of courage, for the North was a lonely country. And he knew that he must be poor in spirit, for he would work among a people who lived a simple life.

In Saskatchewan and Manitoba, he worked with the people, sharing life with them. He tried to show them how to walk in the two worlds: in the ways of their ancestors and, for others in a different culture, in cities of the South. Father Omer celebrated the Eucharist with them, united them in marriage, baptized their children and buried their dead.

Years later, Father Omer was chosen to be a bishop. He now had a special care for a huge part of the Canadian North and all its peoples. He continued to work with love and dedication until he died in a plane crash in 1986.

A young farm boy from Manitoba had kept his promise. He had tried to teach the Great People of the North. In a way, his life was like a lamp burning brightly and giving comfort, warmth and light. The people of the North know that a lamp like Omer Robidoux is never really extinguished.

 How was Bishop Robidoux a witness?

For whom did he witness?

Why do you think he was so strong?

What did he teach the people of the North?

Research further the work of Bishop Robidoux among the peoples of the North.

Select another modern-day witness to research. Choose a favourite way to tell the story of your witness.

Jeanne Mance

A brightly lit cross stands high overlooking the city of Montreal. It is a reminder of the brave men and women of early Canada who gave so much to build this country. Its light, like the missionaries' spirit, continues its eternal vigil over our land.

There are many great women in our Canadian story, but one of the first we hear about is a young woman named Jeanne Mance.

When she was a very young girl in France, Jeanne dreamed of helping people, especially sick people. As she grew older, this call to serve became clearer and clearer.

One day Jeanne was reading the Jesuit Relations. These were letters which the Jesuit missionary priests sent home to tell their friends in France about their work in Canada. "I wonder," Jeanne thought, "if there is some way I could help this new land?"

From that day on, her path became clear. She knew what the Lord was asking of her. First, Jeanne heard of the Society of Our Lady of Montreal, a group of people who were sponsoring a mission on Montreal Island. Then she met Madame de Buillion, a wealthy lady who had a dream about building a hospital on the island and who wished to donate her whole fortune to it. When she met Jeanne, Madame de Buillion knew her dream would come true.

In 1642, Jeanne Mance set out on the dangerous trip across the Atlantic Ocean. We can have no idea of what a transatlantic crossing was like in those days. Just imagine – a sailboat hardly 34 m long and 8 m wide, loaded with people, animals and provisions, tossing around on an angry sea for several months. There were epidemics and sicknesses, food was spoiled and water was very scarce. Many were ill, including Jeanne. But she did not give up. Instead, she spent hours comforting and caring for those too sick to help themselves.

On May 18, 1642, the small band of settlers under the leadership of Soeur de Maisonneuve landed at Montreal, or Ville Marie as they called it. They set up a little altar and decorated it with wildflowers. There Father Vimond presided at the first Mass, celebrating their safe journey and their hope for a wonderful new life. It is probably Jeanne Mance who treasured and passed on the words from the priest's sermon:

"You are a grain of mustard seed that shall rise and grow into a great tree. You are a few but your work is the work of God. His smile is upon you. . . ."

And certainly God's smile was on Jeanne Mance. There in the little camp of Ville Marie she started her hospital, Hôtel Dieu, where she took care of the sick, the injured, the dying. And every day she recalled Jesus' words: "Whatever you do to these little ones, you do to me." People called Jeanne the "angel of the colony."

Hôtel Dieu is now a very, very big hospital. If you ever go there, you will see the statue of Jeanne at the entrance – a monument to a gentle, caring person, the first nurse in Montreal.

Check your library to find out when the Religious Hospitaliers of Saint Joseph came to Canada to take over the Hôtel Dieu Hospital. If possible, interview one of the Religious Hospitaliers of Saint Joseph or invite one to come to your class. Find out more about their work and also about Jeanne Mance's story.

Do a cartoon drawing of Jeanne Mance's story.

Select an early Canadian witness of the faith to research.

Choose your favourite way to tell the story.

Remember
"All baptized into Christ, have clothed yourselves with Christ." (See Galatians 3.27.)

Unit 10
The Church witnesses

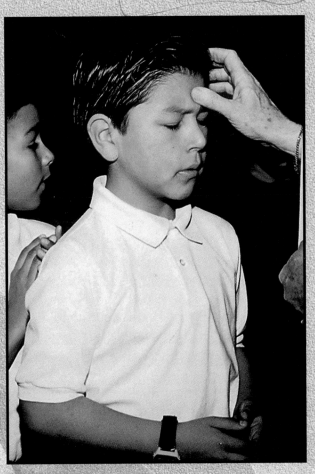

28 What am I to do, Lord?

Paul from Tarsus

This is a story about someone who was very reluctant to become a witness of Jesus. His name is Paul, or "Saul" in the Aramaic language.

Paul was born 14 or 15 years later than Jesus, around the year 10 C.E. As he tells us in one of his letters, he was proud to have been born a Hebrew.

From his father, Paul learned the trade of tentmaking and leatherwork. Whenever he was in need, he took up tentmaking to earn money to live. But his most important work early in his adulthood took him to Jerusalem, where he studied Jewish Law under the famous teacher Gamaliel.

We do not know whether Paul ever met Jesus of Nazareth. If he did, he was certainly not impressed. Paul thought that Jesus was dangerous to his faith. He could not believe that Jesus was the messiah, the anointed one of God. For him, Jesus was an impostor and people who followed Jesus ought to be forced to change their opinion.

Why did Paul believe that Jesus was dangerous?
In what way was Paul a witness?
What does a witness do?

The story of Stephen

B ut Stephen, filled with the Holy Spirit, gazed into heaven and saw the glory of God, and Jesus standing at God's right hand. "I can see heaven thrown open," he said, "and the Son of Man standing at the right hand of God." At this all the members of the council shouted out and stopped their ears with their hands; then they all rushed at him and sent him out of the city and stoned him. . . . Saul entirely approved of the killing.

That day a bitter persecution started against the Church in Jerusalem and everyone except the apostles fled to the country districts of Judaea and Samaria.

There were some devout people, however, who buried Stephen and made great mourning for him.

Saul then worked for the total destruction of the Church; he went from house to house arresting both men and women and sending them to prison. (Acts 7.55–8.3)

Read Acts 6.1-15; 7.1-60; 8.1-3. With your friends, plan a court scene. Have two sections. Section A takes the case for the defense of Stephen. Section B takes the case for the prosecution, with Saul as the spokesperson.

Use these questions as guidelines for drawing up the case:

What kind of person was Stephen? What kind of person was Paul (Saul)? What did Stephen believe about God? What did Paul believe about God? Why did Stephen believe this to be true? Why did Paul believe this to be true? How would you convince others about the case of Stephen?

How would you build up the case against Stephen if you were Paul? What are the charges against Stephen?

On the road to Damascus

Do you know the story of Paul's conversion experience? Look at the picture. Read Acts 9.1-30 and hear how Luke tells the story.

Write the story in your own words in your treasure book. Then get together with your friends and dramatize the event. Use these questions as a guide:

What happened to Paul that changed him? What did Paul realize? How much did Paul change? Why were the other disciples afraid of Paul? What did Paul feel compelled to do after his conversion? How was Paul a witness of Jesus?

To the ends of the earth

Use a map of the Mediterranean world in Paul's time to trace his journeys. Use these details to help you discover how Paul became a witness of Jesus to the ends of the earth!

Euxine Sea

THRACE

MACEDONIA

BITHYNIA AND PONTUS

PAPHLAGONIA

THESSALY

Aegean Sea

MYSIA
Perganum
LYDIA
Sardis

Ephesus
CARIA
Miletus

Athens

ACHAIA

GALATIA

CAPPADOCIA

PHRYGIA

Antioch
PISIDIA LYCAONIA
Iconium
Lystra Derbe
PAMPHILIA
LYCIA Attalia Perga
CILICIA
Tarsus

KINGDOM
OF
ANTIOCHUS

Antioch

Seleucia

SYRIA

Rhodes

CRETE

CYPRUS

Salamis

Paphos

Paul & Barnabas
mistaken for gods

Mark returns
to Jerusalem

Elymas
blinded

Paul, Barnabas
& Mark to Cyprus

Jerusalem

Mediterranean Sea

Alexandria

The first journey

Shortly after his conversion, around the year 34 or 35 C.E., Paul spent three years reflecting on what had happened to him. After this retreat, the apostle Barnabas came to Tarsus to look for Paul (Acts 11.25-26). Paul went with Barnabas to Antioch and from there was sent on his first mission. Read chapters 13 and 14 of Acts to find the places where Paul and Barnabas went.

The second journey ➤

According to the account in Acts, Paul set out on a second journey, this time accompanied by Silas (Silvanus) and Timothy. Read Acts 16.11 and 18.21.

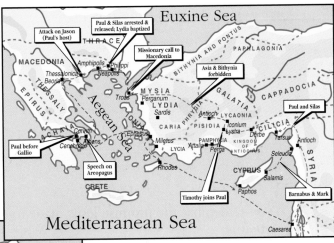

◄ The third journey

Although this third journey is not as clearly described in Acts, we know from Paul's letters that around the year 52 C.E. he spent a long time in Ephesus. It is from there that Paul began to write his many letters. Follow Paul's journey as he went from Ephesus in Chapter 19 and 20 of Acts.

Draw a map of Paul's journeys in your treasure book.

Read 1 Corinthians 13.1-13 to hear Paul speak about love.

Read 2 Corinthians 11.16-33 to discover some of the trials Paul had to endure as a witness to Christ.

What can you say about the great love Paul must have had for Christ?

Add Paul to your Easter people mosaic.

Remember

"This is my commandment, that you love one another as I have loved you." (John 15.12)

29 What are we to do, Lord?

Do you remember the promise Jesus made to the apostles in John 14.3-4? Here it is:

"And if I go and prepare a place for you, I will come again and will take you to myself, so that where I am, there you may be also. And you know the way to the place where I am going." (John 14.3-4)

Do you think the apostles remembered this promise at the ascension?

The first chapter of the Acts of the Apostles records the event this way: Now having met together, they asked him, "Lord, has the time come? Are you going to restore the kingdom to Israel?" He replied, "It is not for you to know times or dates that the Father has decided, but you will receive power when the Holy Spirit comes on you, and then you will be my witnesses not only in Jerusalem but throughout Judaea and Samaria, and indeed to the ends of the earth."

As he said this he was lifted up while they looked on, and a cloud took him from their sight. They were still staring into the sky when suddenly two men in white were standing near them and they said, "Why are you men from Galilee standing here looking into the sky? Jesus who has been taken up from you into heaven, this same Jesus will come back in the same way as you have seen him go there." (See Acts 1.6-11.)

The icon on the next page depicts the ascension: a time of joy and celebration of God's glory.

The figures in the icon are joyful, filled with wonder, majestic.

Christ is in full majesty and glory.

The apostles are filled with amazement and wonder.

The angels are filled with awe.

Mary has a very prominent position in the icon. She is the centre, directly under the image of Christ. This is the symbol of her position in the Church: both mother and member. She also personifies the Church. Her hands are lifted in prayer. She prays for the Church; she prays with the Church. She is the model of discipleship.

The icon includes not only those who actually witnessed the ascension. It includes the Apostle Paul, at the head of the group on the right. Historically, he could not have been there. What is intended is that the Church witnesses to this event.

The Church celebrates this event of Christ's glorification. It celebrates all that Christ has done for us. But our story does not end here, with the ascension of Jesus. We recall that after this event, the apostles went forward in hope to wait for the coming of the Holy Spirit. The Holy Spirit was with them in their mission to gather all nations into one:

"Go, therefore, and make disciples of all nations; baptizing them in the name of the Father and of the Son and of the Holy Spirit.

And remember, I am with you always, to the end of the age." (Matthew 28.19-20)

What's in a structure?

Imagine for a moment that you and your friends are part of a science project about shapes and structures and how they work. You have been given a choice of fruit or vegetables to work with. Your task is to observe and analyze your favourite in terms of shapes and structures.

What's the basic shape of your fruit or vegetable? What does the outside look like? Is it smooth? Rough? Does it have a stem? What's the inside like? Is there a design? Where is the core or nucleus? What holds the parts together? Are there seeds inside? What about a root system? How does your fruit or vegetable grow? What is its name?

Now take your class rock and observe it for a moment. Look at the outside structure. What do you see?

The rock contains the names of the class. Think about your class for a moment in terms of shape and structure. What is its shape? Its characteristics? Now picture the inside structure of the rock. What holds all the minerals together? Think about your class. What holds it together? How are you growing as a class? Do you have a root system?

Take a look at your Easter people mosaic. What is its shape? What holds it together? Where is its centre? Observe the ring-like layers representing sacramental people.

How do sacramental people work together? What is their root system? Think for a moment. What does it mean to be a sacramental people? Share your thoughts with your friends.

Marks of the Church

Did you know that the Church has essential properties that mark its identity? We call them the marks of the Church:

The Church is one

Look at the circle centre on your Easter people mosaic and see the words of the paschal mystery: Christ forms the centre of unity. Baptized into Christ, we are the Body of Christ. In the power of the Holy Spirit we are bonded to Christ and to one another in faith. We are one in giving praise and thanks to God. The Church is built on the rock of Jesus Christ.

The Church is holy

We are a holy Church. In spite of our brokenness and sinfulness, we are a holy people, because the Spirit of Jesus is with us. Through our Baptism, we belong to the Lord Jesus and we gather around his table to praise and thank God with him. The Church is holy in its foundation, in its mission, in its ministries, in its people. God gathers us around the word, around the table to eat and drink. Then we go forth into the world to live out our life in Christ in the power of the Holy Spirit.

The Church is catholic

The word *catholic* means "universal." We are catholic because the Spirit of Jesus gathers Christians together all over the world. From its beginning, the Church in the power of the Holy Spirit has reached out to all peoples. Through the missionary activity of the Church, God welcomes all the nations. The Church is open to all and excludes no one. Recall Peter's discovery in Themes 2 and 4.

The Church is apostolic

Think about the root system of the Church for a moment. Our roots lie with the apostles, the first followers of Jesus, and the faith that they had in him. Remember how Peter proclaimed his faith in Jesus. The faith that the apostles lived and proclaimed has continued throughout the centuries. We still proclaim the same faith. In his gospel, Matthew tells us of how Jesus sent forth his disciples: "Go, therefore, and make disciples of all nations...." (Matthew 28.19) Their mission of faith is passed on from generation to generation.

These four distinguishing marks identify the Church of Christ. They are its gifts.

Research your community to see how people witness to their faith. How do they witness to unity? to holiness? How do they live out the marks of the Church?

With your friends, prepare a litany of thanks for being Church. The response might be "We are the body of Christ."

Remember

The Church is one, holy, catholic and apostolic. These marks identify the Church of Christ.

30 You shall be my witnesses

Flashbacks!

Proclaim
Believe
Celebrate
Expect
Welcome
Act Justly
Reconcile
Love
Rejoice
Witness

 Get together with your friends and think about your year. Create a data bank of activities, stories, events, people. Discuss how each is essential to being Church. From your data bank, choose some that you would like to share during a celebration. Choose favourite ways of sharing your stories and events. Make sure you prepare your own covenant stone.

Preparing a covenant stone.

God, you are my rock

In the name of the Father, and of the Son and of the Holy Spirit.

Amen.

The grace of the Lord Jesus Christ, the love of God and the fellowship of the Holy Spirit be with you always.

And also with you.

Blessed be Jesus
who took children into his arms
and blessed them.

Let us pray.

Silence.

We praise you, gracious God,
for sending your Son to us
born a child of the Virgin Mary.

He welcomed children,
believed in their dignity
and held them up as a model
for all seeking the kingdom.

Make us attentive to Jesus,
so that he can reveal to the childlike
the mysteries of the kingdom.

We ask this through our Lord
Jesus Christ, your Son,
who lives and reigns with you in the
unity of the Holy Spirit,
God forever and ever.

Word of God

"Come to him, a living stone, though rejected by mortals yet chosen and precious in God's sight, and like living stones, let yourselves be built into a spiritual house, to be a holy priesthood...." (1 Peter 2.4-5)

Ritual action

[Name], remember that the Church is built on the rock of Jesus Christ.

Litany

The Church proclaims
The Church believes
The Church celebrates

(All sing "O God, Our Rock.")

The Church expects
The Church welcomes all nations
The Church acts justly

(Sing "O God, Our Rock.")

The Church reconciles
The Church loves and rejoices
The Church witnesses

(Sing "O God, Our Rock.")

Closing prayer

Invite parents to extend their hands.

Let us pray.

Silence

Lord, our God,
out of the speech of little children
you fashion a hymn of praise.

Jesus gladly welcomed children,
took them in his arms, blessed them
and held them up as an example to all.

Send your blessing on the
   Grade 5 class,
on our families and all present.

May we grow in Christian maturity,
and become your witnesses in
   the world.
We ask this through our Lord
   Jesus Christ, your Son,
who lives and reigns with you in the
   unity of the Holy Spirit,
God forever and ever.

May God the Father,
with the Son and the Holy Spirit,
who has shown us such great mercy
   this year,
keep you in his love this summer
   and throughout your lives.

Amen.

Remember… the Church is built on
the rock of Jesus Christ. Go in peace.

Thanks be to God.

(All sing "Go Out Together.")

Remember
The Church is built on
the rock of Jesus Christ.

Acknowledgements

May We Be One, Student Book, school edition revised, is a catechetical program of the *Born of the Spirit* © series, developed by the National Office of Religious Education of the Canadian Conference of Catholic Bishops, Ottawa, Canada.

Approved by
The Episcopal Commission for Christian Education, Canadian Conference of Catholic Bishops

Project Specialist, Child Portfolio
Myrtle Power

Editing and Writing Specialist
Anne Louise Mahoney

Year 5 Consultants
Sharon Breckenridge, Terese Cossitt, Donna Kelly, cnd, Terri Kudirka, Muriel Loftus, Bill Marrevee, Heather Reid, Marie Shewchuck, SSMI, John van den Hengel, Gerard Whitty

We acknowledge with gratitude the artwork, stories and photographs from Jack Croft, Peggy Henderson, and the families and children at St. Mark's Parish, Aylmer, Quebec; and from the following catechists and their Grade 5 children: Carol Bradshaw, St. Michael's School, Trail, BC; Joanne Campbell, St. Augustine School, Brandon, MB; Ben Dart, St. Thomas More School, Fairview, AB; Shirley Gendron, Christ the King School, Winnipeg, MB; Louise Laplante, Holy Spirit School, Stittsville, ON; Darlene MacCormack, St. Anthony's Parish, Bloomfield, PEI; Mary McAllister, Holy Family School, Ottawa, ON; Lisa Nicholson, St. Mark's Parish, Rothesay, NB; Cathryn O'Neil, St. Andrew's Elementary, Victoria, BC; Elaine Orsini, St. Augustine's School, Vancouver, BC; Sue Robinson, Assiniboia Elementary, Assiniboia, SK; Jill Wilkinson, St. Patrick's School, Medicine Hat, AB; Thérèse West, St. Joseph's School, Chemainus, BC; Vivian Zarowny, St. Francis of Assisi Elementary Junior High School, Edmonton, Alberta.

Special thanks to the original Year 5 writing team, pilot team and all other contributors in the field, especially Mary Boucher, Robert Bredin, Edward Brophy, Dwayne Compton, Margaret Craddock, Gordon Dalton, Brenda Dever, Karen Doyle, Ken Gogo, Victoria Hunchak, SSMI, Doreen Kostynuik, Marie Mason, Brendan J. McCarthy, Donna MacNeil, Ken Merk, Clare Richards, Anne Thompson.

of *The Liturgy of the Hours* © 1974, ICEL; excerpts from the English translation of *Holy Communion and Worship of the Eucharist outside Mass* © 1974, ICEL; excerpts from the English translation of *Book of Blessings* © 1988, ICEL; excerpts from the English translation of *A Book of Prayers* © 1982, ICEL. All rights reserved.

Art & Design
Creative Art & Design, Publications Service

Cover photograph
Joyce Harpell/CCCB

Photographs
Photographs and children's artwork come from pilot classes and parishes across Canada except for the following:

Robert Bredin: 101

Sharon Breckenridge: 68, 69

Elaine Brière: 46

Canadian Museum of Civilization Neg. #S88-133: 123

Diocese of Churchill-Hudson Bay: 159, 160

Jack Croft: 147, 156

Gerard Davis: 8B

Edmonton Catholic Schools: 151

Diocese of Hamilton: 35

Joyce Harpell/CCCB: 6, 7, 8T, 10, 14B, 50, 65, 72 B/L, 73, 78T, 79, 84, 85, 113, 119, 120, 148T, 170

Tom Hocker: 138, 148B, 150T, 157, 163

Fr. Phil Horrigan: 42, 150B

Doreen Kostynuik: 51, 58, 59, 62

Le Droit: 104

Terry Lozynsky: 169

Fr. Dermot Monahan: 114T

Montreal Gazette: 162

National Archives of Canada Neg. #PA44737: 161

Mike Pinder: 30B

Clare Richards: 74

Kevin Ryall: 130T/L

Sisters Servants of Mary Immaculate: 63, 64

John van den Hengel: 114BL

Bill Wittman: 12, 13, 76, 114BR

Illustrations
Nora Brown and Eugene Kral

Ron Tourangeau – 166, 167 and end pages

Printed and bound in Canada by
Tri-Graphic Printing (Ottawa) Limited

Published by
Publications Service,
Canadian Conference of Catholic Bishops,
90 Parent Avenue, Ottawa, Ontario, Canada
K1N 7B1

Reprinted in 1999, 2000 and 2001.

ISBN 0-88997-388-1

Legal Deposit National Library of Canada, Ottawa, Ontario